We Have This Hope

Daily Encouragement to Get You Through
Deployment and Military Life

MACKENZIE BOOTHE

ISBN 978-1-64299-124-6 (paperback)
ISBN 978-1-64299-125-3 (digital)

Christian Faith Publishing, Inc.
832 Park Avenue
Meadville, PA 16335
www.christianfaithpublishing.com

Printed in the United States of America

To my military sister:

You are about to embark on a challenging journey. Whether you have done it many times before, or this is your first, braving a deployment is not for the faint of heart. I won't sugar coat it. It is rough. There will be times when you feel like you'll never get through. There are times when you sit in your bubble bath and cry, but there will also be encouraging times when you feel God's presence so near, you will feel like you can take on the world. You will get through somehow, and when you look back, you will see God's provision for you through the experiences you've had and the friends you've made. You'll look in the mirror one day and see that you are a stronger, better person than you were when you started. I pray that this devotional will encourage you, and that your relationship with Christ and your husband will be strengthened in this time. You are stronger than you know.

Mackenzie

We have this hope as an anchor for the soul,
firm and secure. (Hebrews 6:19)

The New Normal

If you are always trying to be normal, you will
never know how amazing you can be.

–Maya Angelou

How lucky I am having something that
makes saying goodbye so hard.

–Winnie the Pooh

Day 1

Saying goodbye can be one of the most painful things in life. When it comes time for deployment, I often feel like I have prepared myself for the big goodbye, but my emotions surprise me when it is actually time. The last time my husband left, I felt in control. I was prepared and confident. This was my fourth deployment. I had this, but when his ship began to back away and sounded its whistle, the blast from the noise made me startle, and I found myself suddenly crying. I looked around at the families with children waving bravely, tears streaming down their cheeks. I lost it.

There are things in life we just can't prepare for. Jesus told his disciples what to expect in the coming months following his death, but they often seemed perplexed. When he rose from the dead and returned to them, they must not have understood why he had to go. Jesus told them he must leave so the Holy Spirit could come, but they had to be thinking, "We just want our friend, the one who walks with us, teaches us, and encourages us." How sad and confused they must have felt watching Christ ascend into those clouds! What

5

would happen next? How would they manage on their own? But Christ left them with this, "Surely, I am with you, even to the end of the age" (Matt. 28:20). We have that same promise. While your husband may be gone, Christ is here is to encourage you, comfort you and be your friend. You are not alone in this.

Reflection:

What part of this deployment am I dreading the most? How has God prepared me for the task ahead?

Day 2

We all have different styles of parting ways. For me, there has always been a buildup to the big day. My husband is purchasing all the necessary items to be away for months, we are visiting Navy JAG to finalize our wills, notifying credit card companies, and a laundry list of other items. We are on edge and snippy with each other when we are never like this. Emotions are high, and every decision feels like a huge deal. I am not used to fighting with my husband, and to be honest, by the time the Big Day comes, I have had it and just want it to be over.

Then there is the drive home from the pier after dropping him off. My mind is running wild. *I can do this. I can't do this! We will be okay. How am I going to do this?! I don't want to do this!* I may start to think of the things he is going to miss: First steps, my brother's wedding where I will have to sit out every slow dance, my birthday, etc. My son begins to cry in the backseat about something completely unrelated, and I am a tornado of ugly crying and mascara streaks.

In the days to come, the hardest part is completing the laundry cycle, and finding things of his. He left them behind because he didn't need them; and as I put them in drawers, it occurs to me that he won't be opening this drawer for another nine months. The ache is almost unbearable.

Girlfriend, if I could wrap my arms around you, I would. Here is the truth of deployment: It. Sucks. There are things I just cannot protect you from. There will be hardship. There will be tears. You know what else there will be? Loads and loads of God's goodness and grace. Matthew 10:29–31 says, "Are not two sparrows sold for a penny? Yet not one of them will fall to the ground outside your Father's care. And even the very hairs of your head are all numbered. So don't be afraid; you are worth more than many sparrows." You may feel alone in these early days. It may seem that no one understands what you are going through, but the One who made you, surely has his eyes on you. He sees you, and cares for you oh so much! You are not alone on this journey!

Reflection:

What has been the hardest part of saying goodbye? How can I depend on God to take care of my needs?

Day 3

I am driving down the road and a familiar Sheryl Crow song comes on the radio. Soon, I am singing along with the repetitive chorus, "A change will do you good. I said a change, a change will do you good..." Wait, what? No, no, no. A change is not good. In fact, it is highly uncomfortable. I mean, if I woke up to ten missing pounds when I stepped on the scale one morning, I could embrace that change, but change is generally not easy, and often requires a lot of work.

This is where I'm at as our family adjusts, yet again, to my husband being gone. It's a shift in responsibilities and emotions. I have to give myself a pep talk every time I do something I don't want to do: take out the garbage, mow the lawn, and change light bulbs that I can barely reach. But Sheryl Crow did not say that a change is fun, only that it will do you good.

Spiritual change is the much the same. The Holy Spirit often convicts us of things that are not pleasing to God in our lives, and we are left with the decision to ignore Him or make a change. Just because it is God's will that we change, does not make it easy, but God will enable us to become a new creation with his help. 2 Corinthians says, "Therefore, if anyone is in Christ, he is a new creation. The old has passed away, and the new has come" (NIV).

Change is inevitable, and we see a lot of it as military wives. I can't tell you how many address labels I have thrown away through the years. It is not unique to us, though, as the world is always changing. Something that is comforting to me, however, is the fact that our God never changes. Malachi 3:6 tells us, "For I the Lord do not change; therefore you, O children of Jacob, are not consumed." Many things in our lives will be fleeting. We will change jobs, homes, states, and hairstyles, but our God is a rock in whom we can stand firm.

Reflection:

How does it make me view God to know that he never changes? Have you ever experienced a good change?

Day 4

I remember my first experiences of being a military wife. We moved all the way across the country, and I knew no one. Two weeks later, he deployed, leaving me with a house to make a home and no idea what to do with myself. I spent my birthday alone and wondered what I had gotten myself into. Things got better, of course, as I became close friends with another Navy wife, and got to know my neighbors better, but I still clearly remember the feeling that I was not cut out for this. I would lie in bed, staring at the ceiling because I couldn't go to sleep and think, I'm not cut out for this. I would jump at every noise, and neighborhood dog barking and think, I'm not cut out for this. I would go weeks with no contact from my husband and think, I. Am. Not. Cut. Out. For. This.

When Nehemiah was called by God to rebuild the dilapidated wall around Jerusalem, he was more than a thousand miles away and serving as cupbearer to the king. He left his comfy life behind to follow a vision God had placed in his heart, and he used unlikely people to fulfill this work. Rebuilding the two and a half-mile long wall would be an "all hands on deck" sort of project, so he rallied the city-folk to help. That wall was rebuilt in fifty-two days, an incredible feat, and it wasn't a bunch of burly construction workers that did the task. The Bible tells us there were priests, jewelry makers, and perfumers out there busting their hump to get the project done. I would bet, as these men listened to Nehemiah's call to action, there were some who thought, I'm not cut out for this. God used them anyway. Nehemiah 6:16 says that when the nations surrounding Jerusalem saw what had been done, they were afraid because they realized God had helped his people rebuild the wall.

We will all have days when we wonder what we've gotten ourselves into. We may even doubt that we can do what is being asked of us. Maybe we feel like we are not equipped, but like the perfumer who picked up a hammer and got to work, God will use us to accomplish something great. We just need to be willing, and rely on him. When Nehemiah was at his wit's end, he prayed this simple prayer,

"God, strengthen my hands." God heard this prayer and will hear ours as well.

Reflection:

Is there anything that I am dragging my heels on that God is leading me to do? What are times in the past that I could see God equipping me for a task that I didn't think I could do?

Day 5

In 586 BC, God was fed up with the constant disobedience of his people, and took away his hand of protection from them. Nebuchadnezzar, king of Babylon, marched in and destroyed God's holy city, Jerusalem. He stole precious items from the temple, and then burned the entire town to the ground, temple and all. The people were gathered up and taken as slaves and forced to move over a thousand miles away. Many years later, a different king, Cyrus, would allow these Jews to return to their homeland and rebuild what their ancestors had lost.

Jerusalem wasn't just any town. It was where God chose to dwell with his people. Before Jesus came, temple worship was how someone remained righteous. These returning Jews knew how important it was to rebuild the temple and re-establish worship of the one true God, so they set to work. When it was finished, there arose a shout from the people, one of excitement and…wait, mourning? Yes, some of the Jews, ones who had seen the glory of the first temple, wept because it was just not the same. Compared to the first temple built by Solomon, this one was a little plain, and it broke their hearts that the former glory was lost.

I think military wives may be able to relate to this feeling. It is easy to look back at our past with rose-colored glasses, and long for the glory days. I married my husband while in college; and at that time, our lives consisted of attending football games and sleeping in late on the weekend. Family was close by when we needed something, and we never missed a holiday celebration. We planned our days to be exactly how we wanted them. We had flexible schedules and if we didn't like our job, we would quit and find something better. That is not *exactly* how we live currently. Okay, not at all.

Nowadays, we base our entire lives on the ship's schedule. We are often separated on holidays, and rarely see our family. My husband works incredibly long hours and misses lots of the kids' events. We move every two years. We never know what the future holds, and my furniture has too many scratches to count. It would be easy to look back and think that my life is not what it used to be. That is an understatement, but I honestly wouldn't trade even the hardest of years in for years past. You see, things are different, but they are mostly good. I now have three little boys, a stronger admiration and love for my husband, and a self-confidence that has been fostered through trials and hardships. And you know what else? I have seen my God move in big ways. I have felt his presence, guidance, and love in ways I probably wouldn't have if I were still living my charmed life. The tough times made him all the more real to me.

The Jews who rebuilt the Temple were faithful in wanting to honor God, but they couldn't see into the future how their work would pay off. They didn't know that the Savior of the world would walk up those same steps generations later. What does our future hold? Only God knows, but longing for the past sometimes hinders us from doing his work here and now, and remembering his promises for our future. When we do his will for our life *today*, we are building a strong foundation that he will use in mighty ways.

Reflection:

What parts of my past do I look back on with longing? How did these experiences shape who I am today? How can I view today as a step to something God has planned for me?

Day 6

I recently started re-reading through the Beth Moore study, *The Patriarchs*. I had done it years ago, and my heart is still written on the workbook pages for me to see where I was at the time. Moore talks about the story of Abraham, and how much faith he had in a time of little direction from God. God told Abraham that he would make a gigantic nation, yet Abe didn't even have one kid. He told him to take off, and didn't even tell him where to. She makes the point that Abraham basically followed in faith until he hit a serious roadblock. Abraham and his wife traveled through Egypt, and he was afraid for his own safety if people knew he was married to Sarah, who apparently was quite the looker. He ended up betraying his wife by asking her to pretend to be his sister and giving her to the Pharaoh as *his* wife. God ended up intervening and causing disease among the Egyptians, and they gave her back, but I bet Abraham caught an earful on the car ride home, to say the least.

Beth Moore makes the point that Abraham should have just thrown the whole situation at God, instead of spinning his wheels on his own. He could have said, "God, you asked me to do this, now provide a way." The study asked for me to name a situation on the line that I was discouraged about, and I wrote that I believed God has called me to be a counselor to help hurting people, but that funding with the VA had been denied.

This study gave me a timely word, in that I realized I needed to trust. I told God, "If it really is you calling me to this, I am going to trust that you will work it out. So do it, please." And he did. That very week, I called the VA once again, and spoke to a different person who told me there was a mistake, and that they would give me one hundred percent funding! (If he can part the Red Sea, he can make a computer system say that they should give me money, y'all.) I now look back, more than three years later, finished with my Masters in Counseling, and working at a fulfilling job helping victims of crime. I knew in my heart God had called me to this, yet, at the first sign of adversity, I was ready to go in another direction.

God has called you to this very place. When times are doubtful and it feels easier to escape, or make your own way apart from Him, stop and refocus. Throw it back to Him. *God, you have called me to be a military wife, and it's hard. If I am going to get through this, it is going to be by your strength alone. Give me your supernatural ability to get through even the hardest, most discouraging day. Help me trust that you will get me through it because you have called me to it.*

Reflection:

What part of my life do I need to step out in faith on? How can I rest in God and stop spinning my wheels?

Day 7

Gideon was just a young man hiding out from a bunch of bullies when the angel of the Lord appeared to him, and called him to something great. Judges 6 tells us that Gideon's people were being oppressed by the Midianites and that they were barely surviving. Gideon is not exactly how we think of a superhero. He wonders if the Lord has even got the right person when the angel greets him as the "Mighty Warrior." The angel of the Lord tells Gideon that he will save God's people, and Gideon objects. He argues that his clan is the weakest, and he is the least in his family. He even tests God repeatedly in the story to make sure this is all for real.

God simply tells Gideon to go in the strength he has. He says that he will be with Gideon and they will accomplish the defeat of the Midianites together. Over the course of the story, though, God tests Gideon's faith as he slowly dwindles down the number of Gideon's army. First, he tells any men who are afraid to pack up and go home. Their army was decimated at this point. But then God further cut the group to 300 men by testing how they drank water at a stream. With 135,000 Midianite troops, it would be clear that the victory was all God's. When it came time to fight, Gideon and his men were armed with trumpets and jars. They smashed the jars and blew the trumpets, and yelled, and God caused such a confusion that the Midianite people turned on themselves. God had given the victory to someone who was untrained and ill equipped, but trusted in God.

I believe we can get caught up very easily in trying to do things in our own strength. This only results in feeling very stressed out. Thankfully, God has not called us to be military leaders and attack a city with nothing but trumpets and jars. But a deployment is nothing to sneeze at. It has its own challenges. Whose strength are we relying on to get us through this time? God tells Gideon to go in the strength he has, that God is with him, and God is with us in this endeavor as well. When you feel like everything is just too much, remember that God is with you, and sees you as a mighty warrior. When you are feeling discouraged, remember that what you have, with God's help, is always going to be enough.

Reflection:

What challenge am I going through that feels like too much? How can I see God's hand in the situation?

Staying the Course
Devotions on Faith

She stood in the storm, and when the wind did
not blow her away, she adjusted her sails.
—Elizabeth Edwards

Day 8

If you turn on the news, you are going to see a dark view of our world—one with hate, crime, and sadness. Politicians are ripping each other apart, refugees are fleeing their war-torn nations, ISIS is systematically killing Christians, and babies are being aborted by the thousands. It is easy to absorb the negativity and get a depressive tunnel vision of our world. But a single trip to the grocery showed me goodness that still exists. I saw a man give his place in line to a woman who was in a hurry, a bagger help an elderly woman, and a woman chase down a customer because she left something in her cart and was about to drive away. These are small gestures, but they are good.

Around us, people are adopting babies, preparing their classrooms for their new students, patrolling dangerous neighborhoods, performing life-saving surgeries, and making a difference. There is not just darkness in the world. There is good as well, and if you don't see the good, maybe you should be the good. What can you do to make the world a more positive place today?

"Finally, brothers, whatever is true, whatever is honorable, whatever is just, whatever is pure, whatever is lovely, whatever is commendable, if there is any excellence, if there is anything worthy of praise, think about these things" (Phil. 4:8, ESV).

Reflection:

What good do I see in the world? How can I have a positive influence on those around me?

Day 9

I love how candid the Bible is in its stories. Sometimes, it will gloss over decades in one sentence, and at other times, will go into detail about someone going to the bathroom or fixing the tears in their fishing net. This is important so we can see that these are real people, like you and me. It is easy to read through the Bible and see the characters as spiritual giants with unattainable lives. After all, Abraham was willing to sacrifice his own son, David killed thousands of men, and Peter and Paul established the Christian church despite persecution and personal danger.

Although these stories are amazing and inspiring, the Bible also frankly states the sins and pitfalls of these same heroes. Abraham gave his wife to another man because he was scared. David had a man killed so he could cover up his adultery. Paul had a history of killing Christians. Peter was constantly saying and doing stupid stuff. Are these details included to undermine their story? No! They are included to show that even heroes screw up and need God's grace and forgiveness. God can use anyone to do his work, and receives glory when we realize it is not the man who was great, but the God who empowered him.

The heroes of the Bible had one thing in common. They wanted to please God. David is described as a man after God's heart. This is encouraging because we can all fit the bill if we so choose. We may not lead a movement, free a people, or change the world for generations, but then again, you never know! God used ordinary people just like us to do mighty works in ancient times, and he is not out of business. He may also use us in smaller ways, which are still important, such as raising children who love him, and showing his love to those around us. Are you willing to be used? Is your heart's desire to please God? Don't discount the potential your faithfulness can hold.

Reflection:

Is there something about myself that I don't like, or believe that it is holding me back? What are small ways I can be faithful?

Day 10

Years ago, my husband was tasked with the assignment of leading a fitness enhancement program onboard his ship. This was essentially a workout session for those who were unable to pass their fitness test. The goal was to get these men and women into good enough shape to pass the test on their next attempt. Brett would schedule a time to meet on the pier for a workout, but he often seemed to be the only one serious about the assignment. Men would show up in boots and coveralls, and even have a bag of laundry with them when they arrived. My husband was always perplexed and annoyed by this display of disinterest and maybe even a little disrespect.

We sometimes do something similar with God. We say that we don't want to do this life on our own, and need Jesus, but we still hang on to things of the past, like guilt, anger and doubt. Hebrews 12:1–2 speaks to this. It says, "Let us throw off everything that hinders and the sin that so easily entangles. And let us run with perseverance the race marked out for us, fixing our eyes on Jesus, the pioneer and perfecter of faith." Have you ever seen a marathon runner carrying a suitcase? Or an Olympian with a bag of dirty laundry attached to him? Of course not! So why then do we try to run the race of life holding onto our grudges and sinful desires? We are not able to live life well on our own, which is why our verse tells us to fix our eyes on Christ. When we are following him, we will not be so focused on ourselves, on our past, our regrets, and our hurts. Our eyes remain straight ahead on the path he designed for us. We can shed the baggage of our past and run freely, if only we focus on him!

Reflection:

What baggage am I holding onto? What do I need to let go of so I can run the race with perseverance?

Day 11

In today's modern culture, we revere people who star in movies and catch passes on Sunday afternoons. Tourists from around the world travel to Hollywood where they can see stars named after people who were famous for movies and shows, and others frequent the Hall of Fames for each sport across the country. This is who society honors as the best or most note-worthy. As far as I know, there is no Nobel Peace Prize or Medal of Honor Walk or Hall, though. In Hebrews, there is a chapter that some call the "Hall of Faith," a list of people who had remarkable faith and hope in God. Abraham gets the largest amount of verses, which describe a life that may sound akin to our own.

What was God impressed about in Abraham's life? Did he kill giants, part the Red Sea, and lead a movement? No. Abraham simply believed God. God gave Abraham a promise, and as far-fetched as it may have seemed to human ears, Abraham *believed*. God said, "I know you and your wife have not been able to have children after decades of trying, but I am going to give you more descendants than stars in the sky. Just believe."

Interestingly, something that is discussed at length within this passage that was counted as righteousness and faith to Abraham is the fact that he was a nomad. God told him to pick up and go, and Abraham did. He did not know what the future held, but he was willing. He traveled from place to place, never putting down roots, always feeling like he wasn't home. Hebrews 11:16 says that he was looking forward to a better country, a "heavenly one."

What can we learn from Abraham? His nomadic lifestyle speaks to me, and the person inside me, who longs for a forever home to put down roots. The unknowns that he faced sound familiar as well. A military family is often operating on very little information. We are called to go, and we go. Abraham marched on because he believed in God's promise and plan for him, and God has a plan for each of our lives, not just spiritual giants like Abraham. Will we trust in God as Abraham did?

Reflection:

How can God use this lifestyle to be a blessing?

Day 12

In my work as a group counselor for court-ordered therapy, I have heard some amazing and crazy stories. It is common for group members to use language that I am not familiar with, and have to either ask the meaning of, or Google when the session is over. One of the phrases I have recently learned is, "Extra." This can be used in a good or bad way, such as, "I shouldn't have drank so much last night, but I went extra." Or someone finding another person funny and stating, "Girl, you are so extra!" It amuses me to learn new vocabulary, and I started thinking about how "Extra" our God is.

Take the story of Joshua, for example. God wanted his people to see that Joshua was filled with the Spirit, so he orchestrated a miracle for Josh to show. God could have just had the Israelites cross the Jordan in boats or rafts they crafted, but God decided that he would stop the flow of the river and make it so the entire riverbed dried up, so their Birkenstocks wouldn't get muddy. The Bible also throws in the detail that the river was at flood level during this time, because our God is extra.

God chose to use a shepherd boy to kill a giant who was taunting God's people. It would have been an amazing story had David killed the giant in hand-to-hand combat, or agility, but our God is extra. David turned down the armor and picked up three smooth rocks, and God's glory was made known.

Elijah wanted to show the people that there was no god before our God, and he challenged the people to have their god demonstrate his power. When it was Elijah's turn, he had the people pour buckets of water on the altar to saturate it, then our God sent fire from the sky, which consumed the altar. That's how God rolls because he's extra.

Consider the story of Jesus. An earthly king who would save his people was what the people of the day craved, but God wasn't willing to do good enough. He sent a child, born from a virgin, after being predicted in hundreds of prophesies, who was sinless and blameless to die once and for all for the sins of the world. That's just how our God works, because he is extra.

See, God is extra so the world will see his glory. He does impossible things through regular people so everyone will know it was by His power alone. It is kind of his trademark. God wants to be extra in our lives too. Will we let him?

Reflection:

In what ways may I be preventing God from being big in my story?

Day 13

Kids who have parents that smoke are twice as likely to take up smoking as kids whose parents did not smoke. It's a startling statistic, given the severity of health problems one can acquire from smoking, but probably not all that surprising. Kids see the example of their parents and act on it. Smoking is something that has received a lot of national attention and research in an effort to inform people of its dangers. However, there are other things we do as parents in front of our children that also have the potential to harm them, even though they don't seem that serious at the time. We may criticize or talk badly about people, or do something dishonest. We may watch shows or listen to music with a bad message. We may be callous about helping those in need around us.

In America, it is part of our belief system that we are free to do as we choose, and it is our right to do whatever we want. While we may have the freedom to do something, we rarely stop to think about how it may affect some other person around us. Paul speaks to this when he states that everything is permissible, but not everything is profitable. 1 Corinthians 10:23 puts it like this, "I have the right to do anything," you say—but not everything is beneficial. "I have the right to do anything"—but not everything is constructive (NIV).

In other words, there are many things I have the right to do, but are they beneficial to me? And how do they affect the people around me? What kind of example am I being to my children? What kind of witness am I to those around me? I don't want to think that something is my business only when in truth I am hurting someone else.

Reflection:

If my kids turned out to be like me, would I be pleased? Are there things that are permissible, but may not be profitable in my life?

Day 14

My childhood best friend and I fought all the time. She would get upset about something and shout, "I hate you!" and storm out of the room. We were both stubborn, but I knew if I wanted to carry on our friendship, I would have to be the one to make amends. I would seek her out, be the first to apologize, and make things right. To be honest, it left me feeling bitter. Why was I always the one swallowing my pride? Why did I have to track her down and be the first to humble myself?

It wasn't until adulthood that I started to think about my relationship with God in a similar way. In this case, however, God was the one constantly chasing after me and wanting things to be right between us. I would go my own way, and ignore him at times, and every time I turned my back on him, he was still there, waiting for me to come around. The Israelites show us this again and again in the Old Testament as they were constantly turning their back on the Lord and not walking in his ways. They would stray far away, but God would hear their cry when they realized their error, and would accept them as his own once again.

When you think about it, what Jesus does for us is the most humble thing a person can do. Jesus was God incarnate, but did not use it to his advantage. Instead, he chose to be weak like us. He had to learn to eat solids and stumble through his first steps just like us. He was tempted in every way we are, and died a miserable death on the cross to defeat death for us. And despite our unfaithfulness, he takes us back again and again. He hears our cry and draws us near to him.

Philippians 2:5–7 says, "Have this attitude in yourselves which was also in Christ Jesus, who, although He existed in the form of God, did not regard equality with God a thing to be grasped, but emptied Himself, taking the form of a bond-servant, and being made in the likeness of men."

Reflection:

What is a current situation in which I need to exercise humility or reconciliation?

Day 15

I grew up in an incredibly small town on a dusty road traversed by combines and Amish buggies alike. On a summer night, the skies are clear and the fireflies are bright. On a sunny day, you can see miles and miles of cornfields and farmland, red barns and horses running like the wind. Everyone in town knows your name, and ladies from the church bring you a homemade meal in vintage Pyrex when anything goes wrong. That was my home for many years until I left for college, and eventually met my sailor.

Military life is quite different. Change is the only constant, and you can't count on much. Our "homes" are fleeting, places we own or rent for a blink, and pack into boxes every two years. It's not easy missing family events and holidays. When people ask my children where they grew up, they just look at me for guidance in what to say because they were each born in a different state, and have lived in several others since. I find myself daydreaming about where we will settle someday. What will it look like? Where will it be? When will we get to commit and not forever be finding those little orange moving stickers on all of our belongings?

This is a natural longing, but 2 Corinthians 5:1–5 really puts it into perspective for me. It reminds us that our forever home is in heaven with our Lord. It compares our longing for a home to feeling naked down here on earth, and reassures us that this is normal, but temporary. These verses end by saying this, "Now it is God who has made us for this very purpose and has given the Spirit as a deposit, guaranteeing what is to come." Wow. God made us to do what we are doing right now, and he enables us through his Spirit to get the job done.

There will be times when we feel like we don't have a home. We feel like we are stuck in a revolving door of cities, assignments, and broken glassware. Take hope! This place was never meant to be our forever home. One day, we will meet him in glory and cash in that deposit for the real deal, a home with no pain, no tears and no scratches on the furniture.

Reflection:

What do I envision my earthly home looking like someday when I settle down? How do I envision Heaven looking like?

Day 16

Taking a shower is one of the only moments of peace I can find in a house full of boys. I crank up the hot water, turn on some upbeat music, and let the steam and shampoo sooth away the stress. Without fail, though, I am always interrupted by someone in crisis. I have a feeling you can relate. Someone will practically knock down the door because they need hotdogs, have gotten a minor boo-boo, which apparently requires a healthy dose of scream-crying, or have a grievance to air about a brother. This was the case when my littlest, Cooper, barged in to announce that Nolan was tossing a stuffed animal around my bedroom and needed to stop. I knew immediately it was no big deal.

"Coop," I said. "Mind your own business. It's not a big deal. Nolan's not hurting anything."

He padded out of the bathroom and could be overheard shouting, "Nolan, Mama says she is going to spank your butt!"

Well, Nolan then comes marching in, outraged. "Mama, I'm not doing anything! How could you say you are going to spank my butt?!"

"Nolan," I calmly stated. "You know me. Do you really think I would spank you for tossing around a stuffed animal?"

A smile slowly formed on his face.

"Cooper!" he shouted. "You are making stuff up! Mama's not mad at me!"

It got me thinking about our views of God. Sometimes, life's circumstances make us take a viewpoint of God that is not accurate. Sometimes, we hear other people's version of who God is and believe it. Be sure of one thing, God does not change based on what we think of him. Numbers 23:19 says, "God is not human, that he should lie, not a human being, that he should change his mind. Does he speak and then not act? Does he promise and not fulfill?" There are times when we feel lonely, but that does not make us alone. There will be times when things are hard. That does not mean he does not love us. When in doubt about his goodness, read stories of his faithfulness. When hurt, read the promises of his word. When you don't feel him, reflect on the times that he was present and brought you through. Looking through the Bible, character after character experienced hardship, and was not unnoticed by God. In fact, he used those experiences to teach, to grow, to save people and nations. It was not for nothing.

Reflection:

How do I view God? Does it line up with his word? How will he use this deployment for his glory?

Day 17

One cold day, I shared a very lazy time with my boys as we snuggled on the couch under a blanket and watched TV. A commercial came on for some weight loss "miracle," and a very voluptuous woman was prancing around in a skimpy bikini. She was pretty much society's example of perfect female physique. That is why you can imagine my surprise when my youngest pointed and shouted out, "There's Mama!" I laughed and laughed. I mean, three kids and a love for carbs has not exactly made me qualified to be a bikini model. I was touched by how sweet it was, though. He loves me so much, so to him that is exactly what I look like: beautiful.

I believe it is much the same with God. Ephesians 2:10 describes us as, "God's masterpiece." I love this wording because it is so telling. Have you ever completed a project and been super proud of it? Maybe you are artistic and have worked endlessly on something to get it just right. Maybe you have redecorated a room and have just sat, admiring it. Maybe you have skillfully crafted a meal, tweaking it over and over until you had the perfect amount of every spice. The verse doesn't just say we are God's creation or project. We are his *masterpiece*! He made us just the way he wanted us. When we get down on ourselves, we would do well to remember this. God doesn't look at us and see our cellulite or messy closet. He sees us as his beloved child, and for all the potential we have in him.

Reflection:

How can I be gentle with myself even when there is something about myself I do not like? Who is God making me to be?

Day 18

I was once following closely behind a large semi-truck as we navigated through a busy area of town. I was in a hurry, tailing his bumper, and my line of sight was only the back of his truck. As he sailed through an intersection, so did I, only to see too late that he was running a red light, and I was seriously running it, with cars hitting their brakes to avoid me. I had been so busy following him, I had stopped looking at the signs for myself. I was so close to him, I couldn't even see that light turn red.

Most of us probably had the experience as children of doing what our parents told us (most of the time). When it came to my faith, I learned everything from them, my Sunday school teacher, and my pastor. What I knew about Jesus was solely based on what they told me. This is not completely bad, of course. The early church fully relied on word of mouth to spread the gospel, as printed copies of Bibles did not readily exist, and few people could read anyhow. It is not the same now. If you turn on your TV, you will find several leaders preaching what they believe, and most American homes have a copy of the Bible. That should make it easier to know the truth, but only if you are willing to seek it on your own. The Bible says that those who seek God with all their heart will find Him (Jer. 29:13). Unfortunately, we are all flawed humans, and the messages we are soaking up from others may not be accurate.

When Paul preached to a group of people called the Bereans, he complimented how they looked everything up that he said in the scriptures, and took none of it for granted. They wanted to be sure what he said was the truth. We should be the same. Many people mean well, but teach things that are not Biblical, or take a wild interpretation of something that conflicts with the entirety of Scripture. When in doubt, go to the source. See for yourself. Ask the Holy Spirit to reveal truth to you in your quiet time. Don't be like me, stuck in an intersection wondering how it all happened. Don't just trust the people who went before you. Trust in Christ alone.

Reflection:

What I am basing my opinions about God and my faith on? What are some signs that a pastor or Christian leader may not be the best person to follow?

Day 19

My two-year-old has real moments of independence, when he wants to do everything on his own, including taking what seems like hours to put on his shoes when I am already late for something. He wants to do things by himself, and this can be bittersweet since he is my last baby. Sometimes, though, out of nowhere he will say to me, "Mama, hold my hand," and we will walk down the stairs, or to wherever our destination is, with his squishy hand in mine. I can't explain the warmth this puts in my heart when he simply wants to walk with me, and wants to feel my hand holding his.

It made me think about our relationship with God, and how he instructs us to walk with him. We can do it on our own. Some days, we think we know best and spin our wheels, much like a toddler fumbling around with his shoes, only to end up with them on the wrong feet. God doesn't force himself on us. He will sit on the sidelines wishing we would just let him help. When we choose to ask him for his hand, for his help, for his guidance, that is when we are truly in his will for us. When we are in his will, we do not have to worry about the storms in life that come, or the obstacles that seem impossible to navigate. Isaiah 41:10 says, "Fear not, for I am with you; be not dismayed, for I am your God; I will strengthen you, I will help you, I will uphold you with my righteous right hand." Take the time today to think about which category you fit in. Are you wanting to do it all on your own, or are you asking for God's hand? Maybe you're somewhere in the middle and can start taking small steps closer to Him. God is our father, and he wants us to be near to him. Just as it makes my heart soar to hold my sweet boy's hand in mine as we walk along, it honors God as we walk close to him.

Reflection:

Am I holding God's hand daily, or am I off on my own? What are some concrete ways I can choose to be close to him?

Day 20

Military families move a lot. This is no news to anyone reading this devotional. Our family moves every two to three years, and many families make huge moves across continents and oceans. While the process is often filled with unknowns, we can generally be confident that it will all come out in the wash. Passports, orders, new churches, schools and babysitters usually fall into place even though it is a stressful experience.

Abraham was told by God to pick up and leave his home with no idea where he was even going. Talk about stressful moves. God did this so Abraham would learn to rely on Him daily for guidance and direction. It is much like the manna that God provided for the Israelites daily when they were wandering in the desert. They were not able to store any extra of it because it would rot. They had to believe that God would provide for them every day.

How do you use your experience as a military wife? Do you trust God every day to provide what your family needs? Do you believe that He will put you on the right path and take care of all the details? Or do you go into problem-solving mode and "fix" everything yourself without even consulting Him? Do you freak out when plans change and things are not what you expected? Proverbs 3:5–6 says, "Trust in the Lord with all your heart and lean not unto your own understanding. In all your ways acknowledge him and he will direct your paths." God knows your needs even before you do and will provide for them.

Reflection:

What things do I have trouble trusting God with? How can I acknowledge God in all my ways?

Day 21

Paul is one of my favorite bible characters. He has a miraculous transformation, and from then on is sold out. This guy risked it all on a daily basis because his vision for his life was so clear. I'm a little envious of his resolve. Paul endured some serious hardships. He was beaten, stoned, shipwrecked, imprisoned several times, and faced danger at every turn. Yet, it didn't stop him from doing what he was called to do. From a prison cell, he wrote letters to churches he was guiding, and he gave great orations that would lead people to Christ while he stood in chains. The man did not seem to be discouraged by his location at all. He would do what needed to be done.

The military life can lead us in directions we never envisioned. We can be moved halfway across the world with no regard for our opinion or desire. The experience usually turns out to be a good one, but initially, it is easy to be upset or disappointed. What we need to remember is that like Paul, we can be used by God *anywhere*. You are exactly where God wants you to be, and he has a plan for your life. No matter where we go, or what we do, we need to be following the will of God in our life and living for him.

Everyone can be of value to God's work, no matter their place in life. You may not travel the globe to tell of Jesus, but you can have an impact right where you are. Being a loving mom has a huge influence on who your children grow up to be and what impact they will have on the world. There are many things you can do from right where you are, such as write a letter, make a meal, or share an encouraging word with someone who needs to hear it. Being faithful in little things is as important as being faithful in the big. Luke 16:10 says, "If you are faithful in little things, you will be faithful in large ones" (NLT).

Reflection:

What little things can I be faithful in? What can I do to have an impact in the lives of the people around me?

Day 22

Being a military wife can be exhausting. When our husbands are gone, we are required to fill the role of mother and father. Logistically, this is difficult, as all the responsibility is placed on our shoulders. We have the regular chores we normally do and the extra chores our husband normally does. We have the kids, jobs, the car, and the house to take care of. The list goes on for days, and the responsibility is huge. The emotional side is hard as well, feeling lonely, being strong for your children, and being an encouragement to your husband. It's so much!

There are days when I wish I could just stay in bed and take a "me" day, but I know everything would fall apart. Who would help me with this gigantic undertaking? That's where God comes in. He's certainly not going to magically appear and load your dishwasher, but what He provides is so much better! Isaiah 40:31 says, "Those who hope in the Lord will renew their strength. They will soar on wings like eagles, they will run and not grow weary, and they will walk and not be faint." Just when we are about to quit, we can receive a second wind, if we call on Him. He encourages us to push on, to do the best we can, and give Him the rest! When you feel like you are at your breaking point, call His name! Psalm 50:15 says, "Call upon Me in the day of trouble; I will deliver you, and you shall glorify Me." Not only do we receive God's help, but we can be an example and encouragement to others with our trust in Him!

Reflection:

What can I ask God to renew in me?

Day 23

When I was a little girl, I was pretty sure I was going to be a vigilante crime-solver just like Nancy Drew. I would out-smart the villains and restore peace across America. I did my research, reading over a hundred of the Nancy Drew Files, learning her tricks, and gaining confidence in each page. As you can probably guess, my vision didn't exactly come true. I did receive a degree in criminology, but that is where my plans went awry. I met my husband in college, a young ROTC student, and my plans were thrown out the window in a good way. He was everything I wanted in a partner: ambitious, confident, a great sense of humor, and a hot car! We were married, and after graduation, he was commissioned, and our crazy military life began.

Are you where you envisioned yourself to be as a child? Most of us probably are not. We may have married a modern day knight, but we probably didn't expect many of the things that have accompanied our lifestyle. Guess what? God knew. Psalm 40:5 says, "Many, Lord my God, are the wonders you have done, the things you planned for us. None can compare with you; were I to speak and tell of your deeds, they would be too many to declare."

Sometimes, we look back, and we wonder what our lives would have been like had we taken a different path. Take confidence that God knew where you were going, and was always there! Today, you are right where he wants you to be, and where he can use you. When the days grow long and difficult, take comfort in Jeremiah 29:11, "'For I know the plans I have for you,' declares the Lord, 'Plans to prosper you and not to harm you, plans for a hope and a future." God has a plan of hope for your life!

Reflection:

How can I look back and see God's hand in my life? What do I believe he is calling me to presently?

Day 24

My grandfather was a Marine through and through. He served in WWII in the Pacific, did three beach landings, and lived to tell about it. His stories amazed us as children. Decades after his service, the habits were still hard to break. He ate his dinner in about two minutes, had impeccable clothing, and made his bed with hospital corners. I will never forget the weekend I spent the night, and he came barging in my room for a 6am wakeup.

"Grandpa," I said as I rubbed my eyes, "Why are you waking me up so early?!"

"I let you sleep two hours later than I wanted to," was his reply.

The devotion my grandfather showed to the Marine Corps easily doubled in his love of the Lord. He spent hours reading his bible and on his knees in prayer. Even in his old age, he would show up to his church to help with maintenance. He was an example that would shape my entire faith.

When he passed away, people at the funeral spoke of his doggedness, his generosity, and his devotion to the Lord. There was no doubt what he was all about. It made me think about my own life, and the legacy I would leave behind. What would people say about me at my funeral?

Deuteronomy 6:5–7 says, "You shall love the Lord your God with all your heart and with all your soul and with all your might. And these words that I command you today shall be on your heart. You shall teach them diligently to your children, and shall talk of them when you sit in your house, and when you walk by the way, and when you lie down, and when you rise." (NIV)

Reflection:

How can I love the Lord with all my heart, soul and might? What am I passing on to my children?

Day 25

Ever feel overwhelmed by the sheer amount of responsibility you have? As a military wife, there are so many responsibilities, it sometimes seems like there aren't enough hours in the day. Martha is a woman who would understand our plight. Introduced to us in Luke chapter 10, she is a woman who thought she could do it all. You see, Jesus was coming to her home and was bringing a group of men with him. Martha would be expected to feed and host everyone in her home, which was no small feat. "Making something from scratch" had a whole different meaning back then. But at least she had her sister to help. Or did she?

Right in the thick of preparations, it seemed her sister had abandoned her, and was simply sitting at Jesus' feet, listening to his words. Martha was furious. She was so angry, she did something quite uncommon for the day. She spoke up to the men in the house.

"Jesus," she said boldly. "I have all this work to do, and Mary is doing nothing. Tell her to help me."

When Jesus replied, He said something that would cut her to the heart, and should cut to ours as well, "Martha, you are worried about many things, but only one thing is needed. Mary has chosen what is better, and it will not be taken from her."

Obviously, we have many responsibilities that need to be taken care of. We are called to be good wives and mothers. However, how many of us have gotten our priorities lost in the mix? We want our kids to be well rounded, educated and well-socialized, and our husbands to be happy and fulfilled, but are we putting so much on ourselves that we are missing, "what is better?" Is your day so filled with optional events that you can barely catch your breath? Is God the center of our lives, or is he an afterthought? If Jesus was knocking at your front door, would we sit at his feet, or would we be too busy to notice? "Here I am. I stand at the door and knock. If anyone hears my voice and opens the door, I will come in" (Rev. 3:20, NIV).

Reflection:

Am I choosing what is better in my life? How am I making Jesus a priority?

Day 26

When I was about five years old, a weekend at my grandparent's house went awry. The weekend was a blast, complete with staying up all hours of the night and eating junk food until our stomachs hurt. They had even taken us to a flea market where my older brother Josh was allowed to buy fireworks. He used up most of them quickly, and as the weekend wore on, he only had sparklers left. For some ungodly reason, he and I retired behind a large arborvitae bush to play with said sparklers. Did I mention there was a draught going on? He lit the sparkler and when it made contact with a small piece of the bush, it made the same sound as when gasoline is lit. Whoosh!

We ran out of there and alerted my grandma, but damage was done fast. By the time the fire department got there, the whole living room was missing. My grandpa, who had been napping on the couch, had the front picture window blown in on him, and blood dripping down his muscular arms. In all the drama of that day, I don't remember them even raising their voices to us. They were concerned about our safety and that is all (if this had been my children, I would have lost my ever-loving mind!). When my parents arrived back from their trip, they were understandably upset and wanting answers. However, my grandparents kept defending us and taking the blame.

Even years later, at my rehearsal dinner, when my brother stood to share memories and joked about that day long ago, my grandparents both jumped in to explain away the situation and how we were not to blame. They just loved us so much that they couldn't stand to see us take the heat.

It is much the same with Jesus. Even though we have all sinned, he took our punishment for us because he loves us so much. He doesn't want us to be separated from God. Romans 8:34 says, "Who then will condemn us? No one—for Christ Jesus died for us and was raised to life for us, and he is sitting in the place of honor at God's right hand, pleading for us" (NLT). Jesus takes the punishment, and intercedes on our behalf against any accusations. What love! The Devil likes to accuse and remind us of past transgressions, but that is taken care of by Christ for anyone who believes in him. What part of your past do you struggle with? Stubborn sin? Traumatic memories? Jesus has your back!

Reflection:

Is there a past sin that I am having trouble accepting grace for? What person in my life has been a great example of grace?

Day 27

Have you ever said something and then realized that you sounded just like your mother? I do this sometimes, especially now that I am a mother myself. The things that drove me nuts when my mom said them are being said in my house on an almost daily basis. Luckily, my mom and I have a good relationship and I look at it as a charming quirk. Other relationships may not be the same.

Many of us come from complicated families with complex personalities. Heck, some families could give Jerry Springer inspiration. We don't always get along, and sometimes there are people we downright don't like. We question their life choices, and wish they would change. They criticize us for our life choices and parenting style. These relationships can be strained or even toxic.

Are you ever worried that your extended family reflects poorly on you? Or maybe you worry that you will be just like a member of your family some day and battle with that thought? Let me reassure you by taking a look at Jesus' genealogy in Matthew 1. Among the genetic makeup of Jesus were Rahab (a prostitute), Tamar (a woman who pretended to be a prostitute in order to get pregnant and trick her father-in-law), David (who murdered a man so he could sleep with the man's wife), Ahaz (who sacrificed his own son to a pagan god), and countless others who worshipped other gods and shed innocent blood.

I believe God used this exact lineage to show us that he can use anyone for his glory, and our family doesn't define who we are. We can be a good witness to them and pray for them, but at the end of the day, we are only responsible for our family unit and ourselves. We must stand for what is right and say, "As for me and my house, we will serve the Lord" (Josh. 24:15). God can use any family tree for his glory and purpose.

Reflection:

How can I show love to difficult family members? How can I serve God despite the way I was raised?

Day 28

I gave birth to three of the most precious little boys, none of whom look like me very much. People remind me of this fact often. "Wow, they look just like their father," they say, and it's true. I am happy of this fact. I love my husband, and think he's handsome, and my children are miniature reminders of him when he is gone. Still, I am constantly on the lookout of qualities that remind me of myself in them. My oldest has found a love for reading, and when I spot him, curled up with a book, I think, "There it is! That's me!" Or when my middle child makes a certain expression, or my littlest scrunches up his nose, I see a glimmer of my family's traits, and it makes me feel even more connected to them. They are a part of me.

I think God does this, too. He created us in His image, and he commands us to walk in his footsteps. Ephesians 5:1–2 tells us, "Therefore be imitators of God, as beloved children. And walk in love, as Christ loved us and gave himself up for us, a fragrant offering and sacrifice to God." God's desire is for us to imitate Him so that we may be close to Him, and we will be known as His children by our righteousness (1 John 2:29).

Reflection:

When people look at my actions and my life, do they know I am a child of God? What parts of me are most like Christ, and what parts need some work?

Day 29

When I was a child and my parents went out of town for a weekend, my brothers and I would inevitably be sent to my grandparents house. My childhood household was strict. I mean, say the word, "Butt," and you would get three days without TV. My mom had no tolerance for "potty mouth," as she called it, and you would never see junk food or soda in the house unless it was your birthday.

My grandparents' house was pretty much the opposite. You could decline to get a bath, eat Doritos like your life depended on it, and be bought fireworks if you begged hard enough, even after the aforementioned sparkler incident. The sky was the limit, and it was heaven to go there, except for one thing. Each night before bed, my grandparents called us into a circle, and we sat as they prayed for people in their lives. I remember thinking Jesus would come back before they were finished. They were elderly, but both were on their knees, and lost total track of time as they earnestly petitioned God on behalf of their loved ones. I am embarrassed to say that I hated those nights. I was so bored and distracted. I just wanted it to end. I look back, now, and as a busy adult, I see what an incredible gift that was. I sometimes ponder what goodness may exist in my life to this day because they were so serious about praying for me and my family. Deuteronomy 7:9 says, "Know therefore that the Lord your God is God; he is the faithful God, keeping his covenant of love to a thousand generations of those who love him and keep his commandments."

Just before my grandparents passed away, their home burned down with everything in it. It was a devastating loss. They had no material goods to pass on, and few sentimental items for us to inherit, but their legacy was the love they showed us all through prayer. Night after night, on their knees, they sowed their legacy for us. What is your legacy? How are you sowing into the life of others? What are we teaching our kids? What are we praying for? In the end, this is the only legacy that matters.

Reflection:

Who has been an example of faith to me? What kind of example am I to others? How can I pray for my husband, his leadership, and other military spouses I know?

Sacrifice

You will come to know that what appears today to be a sacrifice will prove instead to be the greatest investment you will ever make.
–Gordon H. Hinckley

Day 30

I have three sweet boys who are constantly giving me little tokens of their affection. They will make me Lego creations, and give me rocks, shells, and leaves that they think are special. When we go to restaurants, I will often give them each a quarter to spend on a piece of candy. One time, my oldest came back to the table with a piece of candy he had picked for me because he knew it was my favorite. It cost 25 cents, but meant so much more. He had thought of me, and gave to me out of what he had available to him, his one quarter.

In the time of Jesus, people who were lame and crippled gathered by the temple to ask for money because there were no social service programs in that day. As Peter walked by, a man called out to him, begging for money. Peter lived an evangelist's life and didn't have extra money to give, but he told the man that he would give what he did have. He healed that man, using the power of the Holy Spirit, and it was not only an incredible blessing to the man, but a witness of God's power to everyone else (Acts 3: 1–10).

We live busy, busy lives, especially when our husbands are deployed. We sometimes feel like we can't give anymore. We are running on empty. Luke 6:38 says, "Give, and it will be given to you. They will pour into your lap a good measure, pressed down, shaken together, and running over. For by your standard of measure it will be measured to you in return." I know what you are thinking, because I have been there myself. I cannot give any more. I am tapped out. Friend, I know there are days of exhaustion, but I would bet if we all search within, we can find a place from which we can give. We may need to take a look at our schedules and see if everything penned in is a necessity. Do our kids really need swim, guitar, and karate lessons all at once? If we have already pared our schedules down and still feel overwhelmed, there is still a place you can give from. Giving an encouraging word takes a minute. Praying for someone doesn't require childcare. Making a phone call to let someone who is hurting know you are thinking of them doesn't cost any money.

God wants us to help one another, and it is not just for the benefit of the person receiving something. My heart is so touched when I feel like I have helped someone, or encouraged them, and our verse from Luke says that the good we do will return to us! Peter didn't have what the beggar originally asked for, but what he gave was so much better. What can we give to someone this week that will be encouraging?

Reflection:

What is one area that I can give from; my time, my money, or my talents? How will I set my priorities so I can give to others out of what I have?

Day 31

Did you know that God was a nomad for a while just like us? It's true! When the Israelites escaped Egypt, they spent a period of forty years in the desert wandering before settling in the Promised Land because of their disobedience. During that time, they had no official temple, so God instructed them to set up tents and He dwelled among them (1 Chron. 17). What happened when they needed to move to another location? You guessed it, God moved with them. He could easily have been fed up and demanded better. He is the Almighty God after all. He deserves the best, and it took them decades to get their act together! They wandered for forty years, and it would be longer than that until a temple, specially made for the Lord, was crafted by King Solomon. Under the new covenant of Christ, God as the Holy Spirit would no longer live in a building, which would be destroyed, but in the hearts of the people who accepted him.

Jesus himself traveled from place to place, helping people and spreading the good news. He stated that, "Foxes have dens and birds have nests, but the Son of Man has no place to lay his head" (Luke 9:58, NIV). He knew that his situation was temporary and that he had a specific task to do, and so he did not put down any roots, with no mention in the Bible of a wife or family, and no place to call home. Because of his humility, he brought salvation to anyone who would accept it. He had his eye on the prize.

It can be hard to feel like a nomad with no real home. For a while, I thought of the place I grew up as my home, but the longer I have been away, the more that feeling has faded. I have now come to think of my home as an evolving and shifting thing, which is centered on my family and friends who live around the globe. My home has invisible walls and ceilings. Someday, I hope to settle down and live in a place long enough to consider unpacking those boxes that no one has seen inside in the last decade. You know the ones, with seventy-three numbered stickers on them. But for now, I am on a mission. And seeing it as a meaningful sacrifice helps me get past the small closets and outdated linoleum in the rentals we live in.

Reflection:

How can I change my attitude about the sacrifices, which accompany the nomad lifestyle? What are the benefits of living this way?

Day 32

In Leviticus, the Bible outlines the rules for sacrifice. There are very specific instructions for atonement, or making oneself right with God. The best animal was chosen and brought forward for sacrifice. This is part of what made the sacrifice pleasing to God—that it was the best. The animal would have had a significant financial cost and the ritual demanded respect for the details God outlined. This is what caused the rift between Cain and Abel in Genesis. Abel was honoring to God and presented his best, and Cain was jealous because he had not put forth the same effort. His jealousy resulted in the first murder in the world.

The New Testament calls for a new agreement under Christ. He has made the ultimate sacrifice with his blood, so we no longer need to raise sheep or doves to be slaughtered. God still desires no less than our best, though. The God of the Old Testament is the same God of today who despises sin. Anything that we do to ignore his will or his commands is sin. James even says to know what you should do and not to do it is sin. Do you take your sin seriously, or do you blow it off? Are you saddened when you sin, or are you calloused to it? Do you want to please God more than yourself? We still have to atone for our sin, although God has already forgiven it through his son, Christ. This comes through confession, and we can now enter the presence of God with no earthly priest to mediate for us through blood sacrifice. It is no less important than it was in Leviticus to get things right with God so we will not be separated from Him, and more importantly, so we will be honoring Him.

Military families know much about sacrifice; and sometimes, we feel like we've given all we can. In Romans 12:1 Paul says, "Therefore, I urge you, brothers and sisters, in view of God's mercy, to offer your bodies as a living sacrifice, holy and pleasing to God—this is your true and proper worship." However, when Paul calls for us to live our lives as "living sacrifices," this is not an allegiance to our country or spouse. When we think of sacrifice, we must think of God above all. We offer a lot to this country, but what are we offering to God?

Reflection:

Am I giving God my best? What does offering myself as a sacrifice to God look like? Do I try to justify my sin, or correct it?

Day 33

There is a song by Chris Tomlin that echoes the words of Ruth in the Old Testament, and when I first heard the words, I joked that they are being sung by a military wife:

> Where you go, I'll go.
> Where you stay, I'll stay.
> When you move, I'll move.
> I will follow you.

Sound about right? Most military wives have their own career, goals or hobbies, but when Uncle Sam says it's time to go, you pack up and go. Wherever your man goes, so do you.

Early in Jesus' ministry, he called his disciples to follow him. One by one, he calls them by name, and they drop whatever it is they are doing (Matt. 4:18). They leave everything behind, fishermen walking away from boats, and a tax collector walking away from his money table. They give up every comfort to be with him and learn from him. We do this for our husbands—leave everything behind—but are we willing to do it for Christ? What do we have in our lives that are keeping us from him? What are we clinging to that prohibits us to follow him wherever he wants to take us?

Reflection:

Is there anything keeping me from following Christ fully?

Day 34

Military families know the meaning of sacrifice. We often move away from familiar family and friends, have our husbands away for months at a time, and face crises on our own. I have a strong love for our country, and I consider it my small contribution in making our nation run well. In Bible times, God's people had to offer physical sacrifices to God for a variety of reasons. They would sacrifice the choicest animal, grain, or drink that they had to honor God or atone for their sins. The process was written out in the law, and varying from God's instruction would show disrespect to him. Saul learned this hard lesson when God instructed him to wipe out a people group who had persecuted his people in 1 Samuel. Saul decided to do things his way and ignore the specific instructions God had given him. Instead of killing every person and animal, Saul spared the king and all the best animals. Samuel rebuked Saul and told him that God wants our obedience more than our sacrifice. Our sacrifice to God means very little if our hearts are disobedient. In this story, God rejected Saul as king because of his heart.

Similarly, we have to be careful that we are not going through the motions, trying to be "good" people. God is not honored simply by service, but by what our motivations are in it. We can feed the homeless and rock orphan babies to sleep and donate a million dollars to charity, but we are not serving God unless he is our motivation. Many celebrities do good around the world, but their hearts are far from God. 1 Corinthians 13:4 says, "If I give all I possess to the poor and give over my body to hardship that I may boast, but do not have love, I gain nothing."

In Saul's case, he caved to the wishes of his people. He was a people pleaser. He essentially wanted to please the people more than he wanted to please God. I can relate, can you? Samuel tells Saul that arrogance is like the evil of idolatry. When we put ourselves, or others, before our God, we are in effect worshipping other gods. We must search our hearts and be motivated by God to do good works.

Reflection:

What things in my life compete with God? What is my motivation for service?

Day 35

Abraham was called to leave his family, his hometown, and everything he was comfortable with. God told him to pick it up and go, and he really didn't know what the future held. Sound familiar? A military wife is sent on an expedition with little information. You are told you're moving somewhere, and you'll just have to figure out the rest as you go. The Father of Israel was given a promise by God that he would bless him, and that was enough for him to obey. He knew his life following God's design and plan would be way better than being on his own. Imagine what would have happened if Abraham had said, "No, thank you." He wouldn't have received God's gracious gift of numerous descendants, and a blessing on his life. That song, "Father Abraham" that we all sang in Sunday school? No one would have written it. He would have lived his quiet life as a sheepherder no one had even given thought to.

But Abraham was obedient. When he heard God's call on his life, he said, "Giddy up." How do you think his wife felt? The bible doesn't mention this part of the story. It doesn't say that she cried, second guessed, or was passive aggressive to her husband. It doesn't say that she complained about what the weather would be like where they were moving, or the fact that she would have to find a new hair stylist when she finally got one who got her color just right. They heard the call, and they went. As military wives, we know this is no easy task. It is hard to move. It is hard to say goodbye, but the God who calls us will lead us wherever he wants us to go, and His guidance and protection will be with us all the way.

Reflection:

Am I dragging my heels where God is trying to lead me? How can I complain less and obey more?

Day 36

Have you ever not liked someone? Like, really, really couldn't stand them? Through my years of life, I have met some catty, trifling, manipulative, and hurtful people. I'm sure you have, too. It can be especially hard when they belong to the same club, Bible study, or church as you. They may be at your workplace, or even in your family. Certainly, there are times when you need to distance yourself from some people. They may be dangerous or just bring out the worst side of you. They may make you think unholy thoughts. The thing is, most people are a product of their environment, and act a certain way because of their experiences.

I grew up on Mister Rogers, and here is what he has to say about the subject. "Frankly, there isn't anyone you couldn't learn to love once you've heard their story." I don't know if you agree, but I have to say I have seen this in the flesh. For my internship in Professional Counseling, I worked with mostly court-ordered clients who had committed crimes. Some crimes were hard to understand, such as shoplifting false eyelashes. Other crimes were hard to stomach, such as abuse against a child. Time after time, I would read the probation officer's report and make conclusions about what kind of person I expected to meet at my appointment. Then what would happen would surprise me. They would tell me their life story, one filled with abuse, abandonment and poverty, and I would feel compassion for them. The phrase, "But for the grace of God, there go I," started to have a deep meaning for me as I contemplated what my life would have ended up like had I been raised in the homes they were. This is not to excuse their behavior, but just to say that I could see how it would be hard to overcome their situations.

We don't know what pains have occurred in the past or are currently happening in someone's life. Many people put on a good face, are well put together, drive expensive cars, and seem happy while it is all a façade. We never know what is going on in a person's life. I can guarantee if a person's behavior is outrageous, competitive, or combative, there is some baggage there. So what does the Bible say we should do with the people in our lives who are constant irritants?

Jesus preached, "You have heard that it was said, 'Love your neighbor and hate your enemy.' But I tell you, love your enemies and pray for those who persecute you, that you may be children of your Father in heaven" (Matt. 5:44–45, NIV).

I can share from personal experience that often, when you pray for someone you don't like, you are the one who ends up changing. In my prayers, I often find myself being creative about why they may be acting a certain way, and I cover them in prayer. Instead of being irritated by someone because they are abrasive at social functions, I now find myself praying for them to feel comfortable and accepted so they will not go on the offensive. Instead of being annoyed that a person is not taking care of responsibilities with their family, I now pray that God would give them confidence and initiative to seek out a job. It changes the way I feel about the situation and the person. I believe that if you give it a try, God will change your heart toward even the most difficult people in your life.

Reflection:

Who comes to mind as I read this? How can I play for these people?

Day 37

David and Jonathan were the best of friends, which was a an awkward situation with Jonathan's dad, King Saul, trying to kill David on the regular. Saul's jealousy ate at him and made him do crazy things, even throwing a spear at his own son in anger. God had anointed David to be king over Israel; and though Jonathan was supposed to be next in line, he did not follow his father's lead and hate David. In fact, he went the extra mile to humble himself and protect David because he believed in God's plan. I wonder what he went through, being prepared his whole life to be king, only to step aside and insist that his friend take his place.

As a military wife, there are many things you have likely given up. Living close to family, holidays with your spouse, and a career of your own are all things that may have taken a back seat to your husband's career. You may even feel pangs of jealousy as your husband travels the world, seeing exciting places while you stay put, taking care of the laundry and bath time. It would be easy to feel bitter.

John 15:12–13 says, "This is my commandment: Love each other in the same way I have loved you. There is no greater love than to lay down one's life for one's friends" (NLT). A soldier has signed up to put their life on the line and is ready to make the ultimate sacrifice, but a wife's sacrifice is also important. She lays down her life in a hundred ways to support the mission. While she holds down the home front, she makes it possible for her husband to go and do his job, which makes our country strong.

While it is not easy to be humble and step aside to favor and honor another person, it is the picture of Christ's love for us. He humbled himself and lived among us, so we could relate to him. Each time we put ourselves aside for the good of others, we become a little more like him.

Reflection:

Are there things I am bitter about giving up? How can I change my perspective so I see these sacrifices as acts of love?

Rough Seas

When times get tough

A smooth sea never made a skilled sailor

Day 38

Some nights I lie awake in bed and jump at every sound. I ask myself if I locked the back door, and run through in my mind each step I would take if someone broke into our home. By daylight I am Wonder Woman, and by midnight, a scaredy cat. Years ago, my husband deployed to the waters off of Syria during a period of unrest and news channels were showing his ship, which would certainly see action any minute. I must have refreshed a news website every five minutes during that week until things settled down a little. While we do need to be cautious, and we sometimes worry for legitimate reasons, we also need to remind ourselves of some truths. My favorite verse for just this is 2 Timothy 1:7, "For God did not give us a spirit of fearfulness, but of power, love, and sound judgment."

He gives us power to know that we are equipped to the task at hand with God's help, love to endure through our trials, and sound judgment to make good decisions when we are stressed. He gives us everything we need to get through life's tough situations, and He wants us to be confident of that fact. Did you know the words, "fear not," or, "do not be afraid" appear in the bible over a hundred times?

Boy, is that telling. It is not just the military wife who has moments of fear. It is part of the human condition, but we can overcome it. When we get to obsessing over our safety or worrying about our husband or children, we need to remind ourselves that God has given us power, love, and sound judgment, and we don't have to be controlled by our worries. God has equipped us for the task.

Reflection:

What are my fears and worries today? How can I hand them over to the one who is in control?

Day 39

When I was a child, I used to hold my thumb up to the moon and squint. The moon, as large as it is, would disappear behind my chubby finger. I was always amazed by this. It made me feel big and in charge of things. Of course the moon is giant up close, but a change in perspective meant that I could make it tiny enough to vanish behind something very small.

Friend, I can promise you there are things that will happen during this deployment that you wish you could cover with your thumb and make disappear. The last time my husband deployed was coincidentally coordinated with my youngest son's "play in your own poop" phase. This phase hit a fever pitch when one day I could smell poop from the hallway of his room with the door closed. I took a deep breath and walked in, then promptly sat on the floor and cried my blessed heart out. I seriously thought about burning the house down and walking away. It was that bad.

On another day, I took my three kids to a bounce house place. That would surely perk everyone up and get our minds off things. Nope. We stayed for the obligatory twenty-seven hours of bouncy fun, but when Mommy said it was time to go, it was Meltdown Mountain. I dragged everyone to the car. My middle son was crying because he didn't want to go. My youngest, a baby, had started crying because of the racket. Then my oldest started complaining and I shouted at him, "If this is how you are going to act, we are never going to come back here! NEVER!" I screamed this last part like a combination of a scary witch and a person in a straight jacket. Then he started to cry. Not my proudest moment. What topped it off is that, driving down the road, my husband decided to give us our first phone call of the deployment. Of course, I didn't want to ignore the call, but literally the ENTIRE car-load of people was crying at that point. I can't imagine what was going through his mind when I said hello.

In the moment, these events were gigantic and overwhelming. Now, they are just a funny/gross story. That is the benefit of looking at things from a different perspective. I will place my thumb over that junk and feel like a queen. Isaiah 41:10 says, "I am with you; do not be dismayed, for I am your God. I will strengthen you and help you; I will uphold you with my righteous right hand." God is with us in these moments of frustration and despair, and will get us through. Hang in there, and maybe stock up on Lysol wipes.

Reflection:

What has been the most frustrating thing that has happened so far? How may I look back at this differently when a little time passes?

Day 40

Some days when the alarm clock goes off, I open my eyes and I just know it's going to be a bad day. In those first seconds, I hear a baby crying, see a stack of dirty laundry in the corner and have a flashback of the three times I was woken in the night by my toddler. Ugh. Is it really *months* until my husband comes home?

Nehemiah 8:10 says that, "The joy of the Lord is your strength." The original Hebrew also uses the word "helmet" along with "strength." What does a helmet do? It protects your head. So the joy of the Lord protects my head? Yes, and I'll tell you why. We can choose how we live our days. We can sit around in our PJs, watch sappy movies, and cry through a box of tissues while our partners are gone. Or, we can make up our minds to be joyful and thankful for what we do have. Mind you, happiness and joy are not the same thing. We will not be happy that our husbands are gone, that our kids are wearing us out, and that we haven't had a good night's sleep in a month. We can, however, be joyful in the Lord about the big things, that we have a God who loves us, a warm home, and children healthy enough to scream bloody murder. Joyfulness is an attitude that we choose, one that insulates us and protects us, like a helmet, from the bad things that come our way. It is a gift from the Lord, and should not be neglected, as it will make our lives so much more enjoyable.

Proverbs 17:22 says that, "A joyful heart is good medicine, but a crushed spirit dries up the bones." There will be days when you need a good cry and a gallon bucket of ice cream, but a crushed spirit does nothing for your complexion or your heart. We can choose which path we take during this deployment, and our decision will make all the difference. Our desire shouldn't be to just survive, but to thrive, even in the hard days and months ahead.

Reflection:

What things can I be joyful about even when times are hard? What am I thankful for today?

Day 41

Joseph had a life that was full of ups and downs to say the least. He won his father's favor, yet made his brothers jealous to the point that they sold him into slavery. Joseph then found favor with Egyptian officials, being given responsibility and prestige, but it was taken away when a woman tried to entrap him in a lie. He was thrown in prison for years because of her false accusation, and this must have been an extremely dark period of his life. Throughout his story, though, it says over and over that God was with him. Joseph would be removed from his darkness and exalted to be Pharaoh's right-hand man, who practically ran the entire kingdom. Because of his constant connection to God, he was able to save his people from starvation during a draught, and reconcile with his family.

Many of us can relate to a life of ups and downs. Some of us have experienced terribly traumatic events that have left us feeling broken. People who mean well offer platitudes, such as, "It is all part of God's plan," or, "God doesn't give us more than we can handle." I'm not going to embark on a theological debate, but I don't believe that it is ever part of God's plan that one of his children is traumatized, and I definitely think there are situations where we can't handle things on our own and need God's strength.

If you have ever heard the story of Joseph told during a sermon, the emphasis is placed on themes of God's faithfulness, perseverance, and forgiveness. While the dark times are a part of Joseph's story, they don't define who Joseph is, and they certainly don't alter the plan God had to use Joseph for his purpose. I have never once heard Joseph described as a convict or accused rapist, although it would be accurate. No, when we see his story, we see his will to persevere, a heart that wanted to serve God, and a willingness to forgive the ones who hurt him most.

The same can be true with you. We all experience darkness in our lives, but it does not have to define us or label us. God will guide us out of that place because he has a divine purpose for each of our lives. The Evil One wishes to destroy us, but nothing can keep us from the love of Christ. Jeremiah 29:11 says, "For I know the plans I have for you," declares the Lord. "Plans to prosper you and not to harm you. Plans for a hope and a future." There is hope ahead for you.

Reflection:

What experiences in my life am I having a hard time getting through? How can I trust on God to heal me?

Day 42

Have you ever had a day when it seemed everyone you came in contact with was in a conspiracy to drive you out of your mind? I definitely have, and days like this are so much more common when my husband is gone, and I am carrying a heavy burden. Things seem to get magnified by a thousand when I am having a bad day. I'm not sure why this is, but I seem to give grace for the big things, but flip my lid over something relatively minor. Sure, I have patience for people who commit crimes or are addicted to drugs, but if you put your cart sideways in the commissary aisle and ignore me while I wait for you to decide whether you want your tuna in oil or water, I want to punch you in the throat. If you saunter in the crosswalk, fail to RSVP, or take more than ten items in the TEN ITEMS ONLY lane, I am going to be thinking unholy thoughts.

The thing is, this isn't fair. I know I certainly would want someone to be patient with me when my kids are acting a fool in public, or I don't realize I am in the way, or I've said something that offended. When Paul wrote to the Colossians, he said this, "Since God chose you to be the holy people he loves, you must clothe yourselves with tenderhearted mercy, kindness, humility, gentleness, and patience. Make allowance for each other's faults, and forgive anyone who offends you. Remember, the Lord forgave you, so you must forgive others" (Col. 3:12–13, NLT). Ouch. I need to be patient with people like God is patient with me. Other versions use the words, "bear with one another." In other words, put up with one another!

There will be hard, annoying days in the weeks ahead, but remembering our own faults can be a jumpstart for extending grace to others. We are not going to be best friends with every neighbor, and members of our own family may make us a little nutty, but when we remember that we are all God's children whom he dearly loves, warts and all, our attitudes may change just a smidge!

Reflection:

How can I extend grace to someone in my life who irritates me? In what area of my life do I need to practice humility?

Day 43

I recently told my kids that they needed to clean their rooms for fifteen minutes. I set a timer on the microwave, and gave them the instructions, "Go, go, GO!" The younger two rushed to the room they share and started throwing things around like crazy people. Bedspreads were haphazardly placed on their beds, laundry chucked into the hamper, and books tossed onto a shelf. When I checked on my oldest most of the way into the time, there was no noticeable improvement. In fact, it looked like an atomic bomb had dropped in there. I asked him what he had been doing, and he stated that he had used the time to organize his Lego guys. "Buddy," I told him, "you have to focus on the big stuff. Don't get lost in the little things that don't matter."

It is easy to get caught up in the little things in life, and sometimes they actually feel like the big things. There is a lot of outside pressure on women. Fit into a certain size jean. Feed your kids organic only. Commit to making cupcakes for every scout meeting, dance troupe, baseball team, and science club. Keep your house spotless. Have your children in seventy-five point harness car seats until they are seventeen. Breast is best, no, bottles are fine, never use butter, wait, margarine is bad. I'm exhausted just forming this paragraph.

We can't do it all. Let me repeat myself. We can't do it all. Trying to do it all will leave you frustrated, feeling inadequate, and unhappy. And let me tell you something. Kids do not know whether you made your own Rice Crispy Treats or bought them at Target, nor do they care.

There is an old phrase that people will say in books while clucking their tongues, "She couldn't see the forest for the trees." It is kind of an odd saying, but it just means that we need to see the big picture. What is the big picture in your life? It may be slightly different for each of us, depending on what our priorities are. A home-schooling mom may not have the same priorities as a working mom, who may not have the same priorities as a woman without children who has freedom and shirts without spit-up on them. There is a big picture that applies to us all, though. God extends grace to us through his son, and he died so we can experience real freedom in our lives. When we think from an eternal perspective, our concerns and problems may seem a little insignificant.

Reflection:

What "problems" have been ruining my mood lately? Is this a big or little concern? Will this affect me in a year's time?

Day 44

One of my favorite songs that recently came out is by Jesus Culture, and has the lyrics, "Like a tidal wave, washing over me, coming in to meet me here, your love is fierce! Like a hurricane, that I can't escape, tearing through the atmosphere, your love is fierce!" I love it because of the picture it creates, that no matter where I am, how I try to escape God, or my life's circumstances, God's love will envelope me despite everything else.

The creation story tells us that humans are created in the image of God. It says, "So God created mankind in his own image, in the image of God he created them; male and female he created them" (Gen. 1:27, NIV). I personally believe that men and women are created differently from each other, but in ways that are reflective of our creator. When you see good qualities in someone, it is out of their nature that God placed in them. That is one way that you can learn about what God is like, by looking at his creation. When you meet someone with a giving nature, who puts others before themselves, that is God's image in them. When you see someone who brightens every room and makes people laugh until their sides split, you can know that our Creator has a sense of humor. This description of God as fierce, though, I believe women may have gotten a double dose of that quality.

Now, I don't mean fierce as in Tyra Banks saying, "Girl you're working it! You are fierce!" I am thinking more of the way women love their own. There is a good reason that we use the phrase, "Mama Bear," to describe a mother who is defending her young. It is simply in our nature to fight to the death for the things that matter to us. This fierceness is what draws women to foster and adopt children who are not their own, join the military or police force, or fight for social justice. It is also the driving force in agreeing to become a military wife, enduring months alone, and making it work. When you come to a day that is kicking your butt, remember that God created you to be fierce and take care of business. His love is always around you giving you the strength you need.

Reflection:

How am I fierce in the way I love my family? Why did God give women this quality?

Day 45

I grew up in the country with wide open spaces and a sky full of a million stars each night. Now that I am a city slicker as an adult, I am always in awe of the night sky when I visit my parents back in the boonies. I look up and marvel at God's creation, of a wonder we can't even fully understand. Those stars were placed one by one by a gigantic God. We can't even wrap our heads around His size. Some of the stars we look at are multiple times the size of the sun, and millions of light years away. Yet, someone even bigger set them in their place. He created our world with care. If we were one degree closer to the sun, we would burn to death. One degree further away, and we would be too cold. His precision is mind-blowing.

Yet, when I come to a struggle, it seems bigger. I get self-absorbed and feel like my issue is too big to be tackled. That may be true if I were to face it on my own, but my God is always beside me. My boys sing a song they learned at church that goes like this:

> "My God is so BIG! So strong and so mighty, there's nothing my God cannot do. My God is so BIG! So strong and so mighty, there's nothing my God cannot do. The mountains are his, the oceans are his, the skies are his handiwork, too. My God is so BIG! So strong and so mighty, there's nothing my God cannot do."

What is even more amazing to me than God's power is the fact that he cares so intimately for us. Zephaniah 3:17 says, "The LORD your God is in your midst, a mighty one who will save; he will rejoice over you with gladness; he will quiet you by his love; he will exult over you with loud singing." This lifestyle will shake our confidence. It will make us feel small. There will be struggles that are too big for us to handle, but our God is big and cares for us. The same God who placed the stars in the sky has set a path for us and will protect and guide us down that path. All we have to do is trust.

Reflection:

How big is God in my life? What do I feel when I look up at the stars?

Day 46

Some days, we are at the end of our ropes. Our worlds have come crashing down, and it feels like we can't carry on. We may even plead with God that he would just relieve us of this trouble, just take it away. Paul knew this feeling well. In 2 Corinthians 12:9, he encourages those in the Corinthian church that they should not give up, and describes the constant struggle he faced with an issue he felt came from Satan. He says, "I was given a thorn in my flesh, a messenger of Satan, to torment me. Three times I pleaded with the Lord to take it away from me. But he said to me, 'My grace is sufficient for you, for my power is made perfect in weakness.' Therefore I will boast all the more gladly about my weaknesses, so that Christ's power may rest on me. That is why, for Christ's sake, I delight in weaknesses, in insults, in hardships, in persecutions, in difficulties. For when I am weak, then I am strong" (2 Cor. 12:7–10, NIV). Notice that Paul doesn't tell us his specific problem, and I think he does this so we can all relate to what he is saying.

What does this mean for us, in modern day? The God of Paul's time is still in control, and the grace, peace and comfort He offers is still perfect and complete. God doesn't magically erase every hardship we go through, but we can trust that he will give us grace during meltdowns, switched orders, extended deployments, broken down cars, and whatever else comes our way. He also helps us overcome the sin that can plague our lives and take a stronghold. He lets us walk through these things, yet He never leaves us. He gives us grace to carry on. We don't need to be perfect, or have it all figured out, because God is in control and He does His best work when we give up the reigns.

Reflection:

What is a thorn in my side, and how can I trust in God's grace to see me through?

Day 47

Recently, I got the design bug to make something intentional out of our master bedroom. We had moved for the umpteenth time and I took care in decorating my boys' rooms and the "public" areas, but had just thrown our furniture and belongings into whatever space they fit in our bedroom. When I finally got around to doing it, I decided that it was time for some new items. We had used the same bedspread for almost ten years, after all! It was so exciting, after years of hand-me-downs, I would be picking out what *I* wanted. I carefully chose each pillow and sheet, and the piece de resistance was the comforter. Each night when I settle in, I am so thankful for my cozy little nest, and especially that comforter that hugs me when I am alone in that big bed.

Christians sometimes have a skewed idea of the nature of God. They see him as the Old Testament deity, kicking butt and taking names. Angry. Judging. But those characteristics are just part of who he is. Yes, he is righteous and will discipline, but he does so because he is love, and wishes that none would perish. He sent his own son to reconcile us with him so we can be united forever.

God is frequently referred to in the Bible as our Comforter. I love this description because it is something I can visualize. A comforter is something you can be completely relaxed with, safe and at peace. 2 Corinthians 1:4 says that God comforts us in all our troubles. Can you just picture him at those lonely times, enveloping you like a warm, welcoming bedspread at the end of a long day? As we go about our days, he is there with us. When we struggle with loneliness and sadness, he is there to comfort us. He is big enough to cover us completely in his love and not let go. In the midst of trouble, He is there, protecting and holding us. We are never alone.

Reflection:

From where did I shape my idea of God's character? How could it be harmful to my faith to see him as just a punisher, and not a loving Father?

Day 48

Sometimes, something terrible happens when our spouses are gone. A loved one dies, or a parent is diagnosed with cancer. Maybe our child is sick, or maybe we ourselves are diagnosed with an illness. We are left alone trying to figure out what is next and how to move forward, but we are never really alone.

When King Nebuchadnezzar made a giant statue of himself and issued a decree that everyone must bow down to it, lest they be thrown in a fiery furnace, three young men took a stand that would threaten their lives. I'll bet they felt very alone when the music started and every single person around them bowed low to the statue. I'll bet they felt scared when they were marched to the furnace and heard that it was ordered to be made extra hot. I'll bet they were shocked when the guard who escorted them was incinerated, but they were not alone.

The king was shocked to see not three men, but four in the furnace, and said, "Look! I see four men walking around in the fire, unbound and unharmed, and the fourth looks like the son of the gods!" (Dan. 3:25, NIV). It was, many believe, a Christophany, or an appearance of Christ in the Old Testament. When Shadrach, Meshach, and Abednego were at their point of despair, Jesus arrived.

Jesus also did this in the boat during a bad storm. The disciples were understandably freaked out, and there was Jesus, taking a snooze. He woke up, and with little effort, told the storm to knock it off (Mark 4:39).

Sometimes, Jesus stops the storm; and sometimes, he comes to us during it, like the time he walked on water and completely perplexed the disciples. Whether he allows bad things to happen, or keeps them from happening, we can rely on his constant presence. Deuteronomy 31:8 says, "It is the Lord who goes before you. He will be with you; he will not leave you or forsake you. Do not fear or be dismayed." When you are feeling alone, remember that the one who created you always has his eye on you, and will come to you in times of trouble.

Reflection:

How have I felt Jesus with me in difficult times?

Day 49

Have you ever seen one of those pictures where you look at it one way, and its looks like something, and you turn it, or change your perspective, and it looks like something different? There is one with a beautiful lady and an ugly old woman that shows how two opposite things can exist in the same exact picture. Both are there, it just depends on how you look at it.

There is a cemetery that I drive by with my kids weekly on the way to football practice. The grave stones are all flush with the ground, and people have placed artificial flowers and potted plants on the grave stones of their loved ones. For most, a graveyard is a reminder of loss and sadness, but whenever we pass, my little guy shouts out, "Mama, look at all the pretty flowers!" Because of his limited experience with death, that is all he sees, pretty flowers.

We all probably have more experiences in our lives that color the way we see things. Philippians 4:8 says, "Finally, brothers and sisters, whatever is true, whatever is noble, whatever is right, whatever is pure, whatever is lovely, whatever is admirable—if anything is excellent or praiseworthy—think about such things." It can be hard to seek the good in a situation when it feels hopeless, but hard or not, there is usually something to be found. Like the pictures, there exists both the good and the bad at the same time, and focusing on the good will make a huge difference in our attitude and outlook. Deployment is hard, there is no way around that, but there are good moments as well. There are times when people reach out to help, special bonding time with your children, and the realization of how strong you are as a woman. Focus on the good, and see how it changes your thinking. God is using this experience to shape and refine you.

Reflection:

What is there in my present situation that I can choose to see as good? How does it affect my attitude and mood when I choose not to focus on the negative?

Day 50

Throughout the Bible, God has many names based on who he is. Jehovah-Shammah is the Lord who is present. Jevovah-Rapha, the Lord is our healer. Jehovah-Jireh, the Lord will provide. Jehovah Shalom, the Lord is our peace. There are many more. In Genesis 16, Hagar runs away into the wilderness because of Sarah's intense jealousy and mistreatment of her maidservant. Hagar believes that she will die there because she has no food or water, and she weeps bitterly. Guess what? God sees her and sends an angel to comfort and advise her. Hagar becomes the only character in the Bible to give God a name, and she says he is, "the God who sees her."

What a comfort to know that God sees us. Sometimes, we feel so alone in this life. We feel like we are doing it all by ourselves, and the loneliness sets in. We may even feel the bitterness that Hagar felt as she wept alone. The truth is that we are never alone, and that God sees and hears us. Think back on God's faithfulness to you through the years. If you had to give God a name based on what he has been to you, what would it be? "The Lord who _____." Just like God had a plan for Hagar's life, he has one for yours. The days that feel bitter and filled with hardship are opportunities to build strength, resolve, and experience. Even on the hardest day, God is the Lord who sees us.

Reflection:

What may God be refining in me during this tough time? What am I learning about myself in this experience?

Day 51

Michael Phelps was always an active boy, but when his teachers started complaining about his behavior in school, his mother realized there may be something more serious at play. She took him to a doctor and he was diagnosed with Attention Deficit Hyperactivity Disorder (ADHD). With a child who had trouble listening, focusing, and sitting still, you can imagine that there were times when the situation was tough to handle. Debbie Phelps was a single mother and trying to manage it all on her own. Michael's sisters enjoyed swimming, so his mom decided to start him off in it to burn off some of his extra energy. You probably know what comes next. Michael develops into arguably the best swimmer, and maybe athlete, to ever live. He is the most decorated Olympian in history, and all of that started with a rough patch.

Most people experience diversity, and deployment is one of those times when things can just feel like too much. I'm sure there were days when Debbie Phelps wondered if she would make it or question her strength on tough days, but her diversity eventually led to one of the biggest blessings and honors in her life. Romans 8:28 says, "And we know that in all things God works for the good of those who love him, who have been called according to his purpose."

Reflection:

What purpose may God have for this time of adversity? How will I grow and stretch during this time?

Day 52

When I help teach children's church I have a group of four year olds who are fun but headstrong. Part of our time together we spend on the playground, where they line up one by one for the monkey bars. It is a rare four-year-old who has the upper body strength to make it across on their own, so I stand by to offer my help. "Let me know if you need me," I say. Some accept the help right off the bat. Some say they can do it on their own, but cry out halfway across when they realize they can't do it on their own. "Help me!" they scream, flailing their legs. Then, there are the stubborn children. They insist they can do it and refuse my help. They get into trouble, but they turn away my offer to assist. Struggling, they doggedly try to stay the course on their own. One by one, they fall. They are not strong enough to do it on their own, but they won't admit they need help.

We are so much the same. Jesus calls to us, "Let me help you. Lean on me," yet so many of us resist. Just like Peter calling out when he tried to walk to Jesus on the water (Matt. 14), we can call out, "Help me!" and he'll be right there. We don't have to do it all on our own. In fact, we're not strong enough. We are our strongest when we realize how weak we really are, and call on His name.

Reflection:

What do I need to ask for help with in my life? What am I being stubborn about?

Maintenance Period

Practicing Self-Care at a Stressful Time

> Taking care of yourself is the most powerful
> way to begin to take care of others.
>
> −Bryant McGill

Day 53

While working on my masters in professional counseling, I had the opportunity to intern at a non-profit agency which provides court-ordered therapy to domestic violence offenders. At first, I really wasn't sure what to expect. Would I be able to act professionally and keep my cool with someone who had hurt their loved one in a fit of rage? I quickly realized that most of our clients were deeply wounded during their childhoods, most experiencing trauma that would wreck anyone. Part of our therapy was to get back to that time when things were so wrong, and deal with it piece by piece. We also taught techniques for stress relief, such as deep breathing to help someone calm down when angered.

While sitting in on a session with a violent offender, I was able to observe my supervisor teaching a technique I was not familiar with. She explained to the man that just looking up, actually moving your eyeballs upward, taps into a nerve that naturally starts to relieve some stress and calm you down. I could barely contain my excitement because I absolutely love when science and faith collide. God made our bodies with a specific purpose, to serve and honor him and be in communion with him, and he physically constructed us so that when we look up to him, it naturally calms us! (I am getting excited just typing this. Isn't God so cool?!)

Why do I lift my eyes up?

1. *To remember who is in charge.* Isaiah 40:26 says, "Look up into the heavens. Who created all the stars? He brings them out like an army, one after another, calling each by its name. Because of his great power and incomparable strength, not a single one is missing."
2. *To ask for help.* Psalm 121:1 says, "I lift up my eyes to the mountains—where does my help come from?"
3. *To give thanks.* John 11:41 says, "Then Jesus raised His eyes, and said, 'Father, I thank You that You have heard Me.'"
4. *To know God better.* Proverbs 8:17 says, "I love those who love me; And those who diligently seek me will find me."

Reflection:

How does looking to God take the pressure off of me?

Day 54

Kids know how to dream big. Have you noticed that? Recently, my oldest son asked if he could do some chores for money. I said yes and asked him what he was saving for. I thought he would say a Lego kit or video game, but his answer was that he wanted an RV. I will admit, my first reaction was to laugh. He totally caught me off guard. While I know my son will probably not keep that vision for his future, I love that he dreams so big. As adults, we sometimes squash down the dreams that pop up in our minds, even when they could be achievable. We tell ourselves we don't have time, or that we would need schooling, or that we need to focus on just being wives and mothers in this season of our lives. Maybe we are stuck in a job and we feel that leaving would be too risky.

God gives each of us passions, and they may lead us to serving Him in a new way, but they may just be pleasing to us. David was a beautiful harp player, so much so that he was requested to play to soothe King Saul, which was the catalyst of God using him to kill Goliath. Foremost, he was a shepherd, so can you imagine if David said, "The only thing I will do for the rest of my life is herd animals. I need to focus on these sheep with every minute I have," he would never have learned to play the harp, which was his "in" with the King. We need to find a balance in our lives. God has given us responsibilities, yes, but he also desires us to have pleasure, and out of this pleasure often comes worship. When we are being who God designed us to be, it is the greatest form of worship. What passion are you putting on the back burner? Who did God make you to be? "Delight yourself in the Lord, and He will give you the desires of your heart" (Ps. 37:4).

Reflection:

Is there a dream God has placed on my heart? How can I balance my responsibilities with my dreams?

Day 55

When the Israelites were fighting the Amalekites, a group of people who had attacked them, Moses sat on a hilltop watching the battle. He clutched the staff of God in his hands, and when he held his hands high, the Israelites were winning the war. However, when he began to tire, the staff would lower and the Israelites would begin to lose. The solution was clear to Moses' brother, Aaron, and their friend, Hur. They got on either side of Moses and propped up his arms to ensure the victory. Moses was a holy man and a fantastic leader anointed by God, yet he couldn't do it all by himself. Even he needed the help of those close to him to succeed in his endeavors.

We don't always know why God does the things he does. God is all powerful. He could have said the word, and the Amalekites would have been wiped from the face of the earth. Instead, he chose to let his people fight. Even then, he didn't simply hand them the victory. It was Moses' diligence in raising his arms that gave the Israelites God's power, and the faithfulness of his comrades to see him through the struggle.

Being in the military is no easy task. So often, our husbands are asked to do tasks that cannot be done alone. No matter the amount of courage, dedication, or heart of your husband, these tasks are made easier when there is someone they can count on to support them.

You may sometimes feel isolated in your role as military wife. You are often alone, left behind to make the best of a difficult situation. But you are doing more than just holding down the home front. You are also holding up the arms of your husband, stabilizing his life and making what he does possible. Everyday routines like paying the bills, mowing the lawn, taking your children to school, and listening to his concerns and complaints enable him to perform the job he's been called to. With the assistance of your faithful presence, your husband will be able to stand firm and fight through every challenge, and every battle. In the meantime, it is also important to identify the friends and family who will hold up your arms during this deployment.

Reflection:

Who is there to support me? If it feels like I am alone, where can I acquire support from?

Day 56

I have recently tested my fortitude by entering back into the world of work, by way of an internship. It's not that many hours a week, maybe twenty-five, but with finishing my masters in counseling and being a mom with three boys on three different baseball teams, I can assure you it has its moments. I certainly don't mean that in the good sense, although it is rewarding and exhilarating. I mean the moments where I feel like I may have to check myself in for a mental health evaluation at the facility where I work.

There are days I have forgotten very important things, such as when I provided NO TREAT for my son's sixth birthday at school. He took it in stride, but man, that guilt ate at me. There are often dishes piled high in the sink, and we are always scrambling to find socks to wear before the bus speeds past us. I find myself thinking, *If I just had one day to catch up, if I could just get it together…*

It's a nice thought, and truly, if I do get a free day to do laundry and grocery shop, it feels heavenly. But you know what? The next day is back to chaos. I can never truly "catch up." These children are like Tasmanian Devils. I feel like I am failing at the very basic things in my life, and the stress of living in a disaster area makes me wonder if my husband is considering running away with a Merry Maids employee. I bet she has an orderly home.

The good news is that Jesus doesn't expect me to have it all together. In fact, he knows I don't, and it's why he came to this earth. He said that everything boils down to two commandments, and gratefully, they are not, "Thou shalt not feed your kids Chick-fil-A again," and, "Thou shalt not make your child wear dirty baseball pants to his game." He said we are to love God, and love others (Matt. 22:37–38).

It's easy to get lost in the busyness of our everyday lives. Homework. Dinner. Work. Jesus does not give these commandments to add one more thing to the list. *Oh, great, I have so much to do, and now he wants me to feel guilty about how much I love people?* Nope, he's saying it's pretty much the only thing that matters. He's taking the rest of your to-do list and tearing it up into tiny squares (and maybe doing some David Copperfield-like trick thingy to make it disappear because this cat is cool). Of course we have responsibilities, but we don't have to have it all together. No one does! How are we loving God and loving others? That is what matters.

Reflection:

What things are taking up time in my life which are unnecessary, and are not life-giving to me? What is one specific way I can love God and love others this week?

Day 57

This New Year's, I made an anti-resolution. Have you ever seen the movie, "Yes Man" with Jim Carey? The central plot is that he has to say "yes" to whatever is put before him. Skydiving? Learning Korean? Playing the guitar? Yes, yes, and yes. I can be a little like this in real life. I am the creative sort, and I will get some pretty zany aspirations for my life, most of which I don't have the time for. When someone asks me to volunteer, be a part of some committee, or bake a billion cookies for my child's class, I say yes, yes, yes. Of course I mean well. I want to be helpful. But the problem is, I get strung out. I even lose quality time with my own family as a result. There were nights I was working on "busy work" projects and I had to run through a drive-thru to feed my kids. I then crammed food in my face so I could get back to work quickly.

So this year, I said no. In fact, I made a resolution that my first response when asked to participate in something was either a flat out no or that I would think about it and get back to them. Giving back to your community or your kid's school is a wonderful thing. It feels good to help. But so many times we are doing too much. We are frazzled, we are yelling at our kids, we are rushing place to place, and for what? So some second graders have handmade cupcake toppers? So you can plan pajama day with the PTA? So we can ensure that things are being done exactly how we want them done? There are good opportunities to serve, but when we are stressed and already overextended, sometimes we need to say no. The good thing is, the more we say it, the easier it becomes. One thing is for sure, the projects we do take on need to be glorifying of God. Are we being a good witness to our families or those around us if we are frustrated, ill tempered, and cranky while doing our tasks? Colossians 3:17 tells us that whatever we do should be done for the glory of God. If there is any question, perhaps our answer should be no.

Reflection:

What do I need to say no to? How will I be diligent to listen to God before saying yes?

Day 58

As a therapist, insurance insists that you give a diagnosis to someone on the very first time talking with them. It is an ethical concern, in my opinion, but that is how the system is set up. Someone walks into your door, shares some symptoms, and boom! A label is slapped on them, which may follow them the rest of their lives.

In the human trafficking world, which is permeating our society more and more, a pimp often changes the name of the trafficked women to dehumanize and claim ownership. It is a symbol that your old life is gone, and now you belong to them. Oftentimes, tattoos are forced on young women so they are branded like cattle.

God often renamed people in the Bible, but the effect was the opposite. He saw the good in people, and wanted to draw attention to it. He also renames us out of ownership, but because he is proud of us, and wants to claim us as his legitimate children. He renamed Jacob, whose name, "Heel-grabber," basically pointed out that he was conniving and trying to get what was not rightfully his. He was given this name by his parents, who witnessed that he was grabbing the heel of his brother while being born. As you probably know, he tricked this same brother into forfeiting his birthright, and deceived his father into giving him a blessing that did not belong to him.

God changed Jacob's name and gave him the name Israel, and the descendants of Jacob became the lineage of Christ. God saw the potential, not the weakness in Jacob. What labels have others put on you? What labels have you put on yourself? No matter what they are, or how harmful they are, God has placed his own label on you, and it says, "Mine." He is proud of you, and loves you.

> For you created my inmost being; you knit me together in my mother's womb. I praise you because I am fearfully and wonderfully made;

your works are wonderful, I know that full well.
(Ps. 139:13–14, NIV)

Reflection:

What labels do you wear? Who gave you these labels? How does God see you?

Day 59

I have come to mark time by seasons in my life, and not years. It helps me to be patient. You see, there are seasons of pregnancy, of breastfeeding, sleepless nights, and poopie diapers. It feels like it will last forever, and then in a blink, your kids are school age. The season is over, and you are moving on to new blessings and challenges. It is like this with all of life. Sometimes the seasons are trying or heartbreaking: Ill loved ones, a rough patch in your marriage, or a deployment. You do what you can to take care of yourself in these times, and lean in to God who knows your struggle and will comfort you. A season, just like falling leaves in autumn or snowy streets in winter, eventually passes and ushers in a new time.

Ecclesiastes 3 says there is a season for everything. "There is a time for everything, and a season for every activity under the heavens:

> a time to be born and a time to die,
> a time to plant and a time to uproot,
> a time to kill and a time to heal,
> a time to tear down and a time to build,
> a time to weep and a time to laugh,
> a time to mourn and a time to dance,
> a time to scatter stones and a time to gather them,
> a time to embrace and a time to refrain from embracing,
> a time to search and a time to give up,
> a time to keep and a time to throw away,
> a time to tear and a time to mend,
> a time to be silent and a time to speak,
> a time to love and a time to hate,
> a time for war and a time for peace."

For a military wife, these things all apply. I may want to add in a few, though. A time to cry in frustration, and a time to throw off the covers and seize the day. A time to have a mini-pity party, and a time to kick yourself in the butt and get in gear. A time to eat a tub of ice cream and a time to be conscientious about your health. A time to make a homemade feast for your kids, and a time for the drive-thru. It is all a balancing act. Like the waves in the ocean, there is a crest and a trough. There will be ups and downs in this deployment. The good news is that the hard times do not last forever. There will be a reprieve when things are under control and you feel good. Thinking about this time as a passing season may help get through it. There will be an end, and what follows it is a sweet season of self-confidence and reconnection with your spouse. Focus on getting through today, and you will see.

Reflection:

What season of life am I in right now? How can I embrace this time and grow in the midst of it?

Day 60

I love helping people. There is something that feels so good when you do something nice for someone, especially if they are surprised by it. Sometimes, though, the timing is off when someone is in need, and I feel anxious and obligated. So-and-so just had a baby, I should make her a meal. My son's class is having a party, I should take off work and bring cupcakes. A neighbor's child was diagnosed with cancer, I should organize a fundraiser. The problem is, life gets in the way, and I can't do everything, especially when my husband is deployed. These are all great causes, but there are always going to be a zillion great causes because life has struggles such as sickness; and excitement, such as the birth of a baby and parties. I simply cannot do everything for everyone every time.

So what's a girl to do? First, consider that this is a time that you will just say no. There's no shame in this. We certainly have a lot on our plate. However, if you are feeling like going above and beyond, pray about it. Does God even want me involved in this? We will have to discern what God is calling us to, and what is just the PTA President for the zillionth time. There is a time to extend ourselves and a time to be wise and kindly say no. I have found, on those times, where I have not consulted God and did something in my own strength, that I was bitter about the task. Take for example the time I was asked to bake hundreds of cookies at Christmastime for my husband's command. From the outset, I knew it was bad timing do it, but I still said yes. I was stressed the entire time I baked, barking at my kids not to touch anything, and using precious time that could have been spent on my family's own traditions. I literally had a bad attitude during the entire process. Is that the kind of sacrifice God desires? I doubt it.

What if God gives the go-ahead? The God we serve is one of miracles. When they ran out of wine at the wedding in Cana, Jesus took a simple offering of water and multiplied it to become a wine so delicious, the guests thought the host had saved the best for last. When Jesus had compassion on a group that had been clinging to his every word for days and were hungry, he multiplied some small loaves and a fish to feed five thousand people.

Our offerings can be the same. We may feel that we are tapped out and have no more to give, but we can trust that if God calls us to do something, he can and will make it great for his purpose. Something as simple as a written card or phone call can mean the world to someone when it is well-timed. When God calls us to something, he will also provide the strength and energy we need to perform the task, even on days where we feel like we have nothing left to give.

Reflection:

How will I be wise about my use of time? How will I rely on God to give me the strength to help others?

Thankfulness

The miracle of gratitude is that it shifts your perception
to such an extent that it changes the world you see.
　　　　　　　　　　　　　　　　　　　　–Dr. Robert Holden

Day 61

It was recently my honor to go on a mission trip to El Salvador. I thought I was ready, but nothing could prepare me for the exposure to the abject poverty and sadness that existed there. I saw children sleeping with no blankets in the streets, and their faces pressed against the cold sidewalk. I saw teenagers locked in an orphanage for being too badly behaved after years of savage abuse at the hands of adults. I watched a boy, the age of my son, begging for food, stoned out of his mind from sniffing glue.

These sights were overwhelming, to be honest. I had so many emotions at once. I felt some guilt about the relatively posh lifestyle I enjoy in the States, I felt sadness that kids were living this way, and I felt outrage that people didn't care enough about their plight to remove them from this hell.

During our time there, our group built a home for a young man and his family who was a former gang member. His life was in jeopardy because he had decided to leave the gang when he became a follower of Christ. When we finished the home, we dedicated it to God, and prayed over the family. The leader of our group, who lives in El Salvador full time, prayed for them in this life, but mostly emphasized the afterlife to come for them. They might not experience many good things in this life, after all.

People in El Salvador and other places like it have a very different perspective from those of us who live in the U.S. They are focused on heaven and crave it on a daily basis because their current situation is so dire. They crave God in a way we can't relate to because they don't know when they will next eat or if they will be safe tonight. We complain about things like slow wireless and not having something to wear when we have a closet full of clothes. I wonder how my life would be different if I chose an eternal perspective every day. How would I spend my time and money? What would I be thankful for? What would become important, and what would I see as no big deal?

> My Father's house has many rooms; if that were not so, would I have told you that I am going there to prepare a place for you? And if I go and prepare a place for you, I will come back and take you to be with me that you also may be where I am. (John 14:2–3, NIV)

Reflection:

How can I be intentional about focusing on an eternal perspective?

Day 62

I sometimes have waves of jealousy wash over me like the ocean laps at the seashore. I wouldn't normally describe myself as a jealous person, but if I am honest with myself, I experience it from time to time. You see, I often find myself comparing people and situations and stewing a little. I might look out at the bus stop in the morning and see a father with his child and wonder, what time does he have to be at work? My husband left hours ago. Or I may see lovely pictures of a friend's family vacation on Facebook and think, I wish we had the opportunity to take a trip together, but my husband can't get off work. Instead of just being happy for them, I find myself thinking, why not me? Comparing different families is comparing apples and oranges to say the least, and one thing is certain: It will steal your joy. When we covet what others have, we are essentially saying that we are not pleased with what we have. We are throwing our blessings in God's face and whining like a two year old saying, "I want more!"

As I write this, someone I know is waking up to the realization that her ten year old daughter is living her last days. Her tumors are not shrinking with even the most aggressive treatments, and her little life is slipping away. Hospice will be called in, and the only thing to be done is to make her comfortable until she passes from this world.

Why do we rarely compare our lives to a situation such as this? We want to look around and see how good everyone has it, like the whole world has won the lottery and we are out of luck, but we are blind to how blessed we really are. We ask, why can't I have nicer car, vacation, hot shoes, or new furniture? We should be asking, why was my child spared? Why are my children healthy? Why was I born in America, and not some poverty-stricken, war-torn nation? Why does God continually bless me?

I do not mean to diminish the true and hard sacrifice that military life is, however, there is always a blessing to be discovered in every situation, and we need to recognize them and give thanks so we don't become spiteful and jealous. Psalm 9:1–2 says, "I will give thanks to the Lord with my whole heart; I will recount all of your wonderful deeds. I will be glad and exult in you; I will sing praise to your name, O Most High."

Reflection:

How will I keep from becoming jealous when it is my first instinct? How will I be thankful with my whole heart?

Day 63

I made a large tray of cookies one day and foolishly placed them at eye-level of my two-year-old son. He started scarfing them down, and I quickly saw he had no self-control and would eat them until he exploded if I let him. As he ate the cookie stuffed in his little chipmunk cheeks, I gave him one to hold in his hands, and told him that was all he was getting. Like a normal two-year-old, he started to fuss and reach and jump for the tray I had now put up. I had to laugh. His mouth was so full of cookie he couldn't shut his lips all the way, and he still had another cookie in his hand, but it wasn't enough. He wanted them all, and hated the feeling that I was holding something back from him.

I am sometimes like this with God. I have so many blessings, but sometimes find myself dwelling on what I don't have. I wish I could travel more. I wish I had more alone time with my husband. Sometimes, I wish my husband had chosen a different career as I see the neighbors' husbands all return home at reasonable hours in the evening and I feel a pang of jealousy. Sure, I have some great things in my life, too many to count really, but there are days when it feels like someone is keeping a tray of cookies from me. Know what I mean?

The Bible tells us to be content with what we have. Being discontent is the pitfall of so many people within its pages. God's anger raged against the Israelites when they grumbled about their conditions in the desert. He provided for them constantly, but they thought they deserved more. We may read these stories and scoff at their selfishness, but at times, we are no different. Proverbs 14:30 says that, "A tranquil heart gives life to the flesh, but envy makes the bones rot." Well, that is both a comfort and a warning. It is true that envy and discontentedness will eat at us. What is the antidote? Thankfulness. Count your blessings and your contentment will grow and grow.

Reflection:

In what ways have I been discontent recently? How can I be more content?

Day 64

Some days, everything is going right for me. I get my son on the bus in time with a real breakfast in his belly, I start a load of laundry, get my quiet time in with God, and have a cup of coffee before the other two even wake. My hair in on point. I am a well-oiled machine, efficient and confident. I am polishing my Mommy of the Year Award on the mantle. Then it happens. Everything falls apart. Someone smears poop all over a wall, the toilet is clogged—AGAIN, I am running late for an appointment, and everyone is crying all at once, and for no apparent reason. All of a sudden, I am stressed. I'm barking out orders, yelling at the kids, and wondering if I can put them to bed at four in the afternoon.

Life can be crazy, and with children, it can be so unpredictable. For a while it seemed like every time we started a long road trip, someone decided to get molars or become violently ill in our minivan. Sometimes, we get caught up in the moment, and we forget how fleeting time is, and a momentary frustration makes us say or do things that are inappropriate. We neglect to be thankful for all God has given us. We feel frazzled, stressed, angry, or overwhelmed when we take our focus off him. In years to come, we will think back on these days with a smile. In the meantime, we need to focus on God and remind ourselves that, "We can do all things through Him who gives us strength" (Phil 4:13, NIV). The Holy Spirit offers peace, patience, kindness, goodness, and self-control. When you feel overwhelmed, remember that you are not alone. You can tap into the power of the Spirit and march on.

Reflection:

How can I change my self-talk in frustrating situations? What three things am I thankful for today?

Day 65

I love the "Debbie Downer" skit that Saturday Night Live used to do. If you're not familiar with it, YouTube it immediately. (You're welcome!) Debbie Downer is a woman who has a knack for making every situation depressing. At Thanksgiving dinner, she brings up tragic stories and turns every conversation to something sad. She is the bearer of bad news—always. I think she resonates with me because she is so relatable. I would be willing to bet we each have someone like this in our lives. Worse yet, some days, we may even be Debbie Downer ourselves.

Deployment is rough, there's no doubt about it. Your emotions will run the gamut from fear, sadness, frustration, anger, jealousy, and exhaustion. And that's just before lunch! However, dwelling on these feelings isn't healthy for anyone, especially you. Philippians 4:8 says, "Finally, brothers and sisters, whatever is true, whatever is noble, whatever is right, whatever is pure, whatever is lovely, whatever is admirable—if anything is excellent or praiseworthy—think about such things."

When times are tough, don't wallow in your misery. And don't take the ship down with you, so to speak. Find something that is good and focus on that. For instance, I can thank God my husband has a job, that I have these amazing children, and that I have friends who love me. The verse even suggests that thinking about lovely things is helpful. Take a trip to the beach, sit outside, or go to a museum. Take in God's beauty. If we focus on things that are excellent and praiseworthy, we are less likely to be Debbie Downer.

Reflection:

What can I choose to be more positive about? What are the true, noble, right, pure, lovely and admirable things in my life?

Day 66

As the mother of three boys, things seldom go as planned in my house. Just as I get ready to leave, someone pees in their pants, and one is crying because the other took a toy away. There are piles of laundry and dishes, and no clean pants for baseball practice. There's homework to do, and no sharpened pencil to be found in the whole house. My children have actually wrestled over a piece of paper. I have seen bad days. I have cried in frustration. What is important to remember, though, is that every day, even a bad one, has been made by God and ordained for a purpose.

Psalm 118:24 says, "This is the day the Lord has made. I will rejoice and be glad in it!" There will be days when you feel like pulling your hair out. (Can I get an amen?) What is important is to not let that be your entire focus. There is so much that is right, too.

Ann Voskamp wrote an entire book called *One Thousand Gifts,* which encourages women to ponder three specific gifts that God has given each day. She writes about how an attitude of appreciation actually changes our lives and makes us more grateful and aware of all God does for us. Making this a practice for a whole year will result in a list of more than 1000 things that God has given us. They may be small, such as iridescent bubbles in the sink, or a chirping bird, and they may be big, such as the fact that God made the tides so that we are not flooded and wiped out with the pull of the moon. Stop and thank God for those things, big and little, and it will help refocus your day. These hard days are making you stronger, and giving you stories to tell when your children are grown and embarrassing pictures to show future girlfriends!

Reflection:

What can I thank God for today? What are the big and small ways he has blessed my life?

Day 67

I took a nice, hot shower this morning. You probably did, too. My husband calls it a "Hollywood" when someone takes a shower that lasts longer than two minutes, which was the time they were allotted in boot camp. The shower is my sanctuary. It is pretty much the only place I can concentrate without kids tattling on one another and asking for ridiculous amounts of chocolate milk. I pray in there, worship in there, plan my day in there, and pretty much solve the world's problems in there. This time became all the more precious to me when our hot water heater broke and I was left with very *not* hot water. In fact, I was without for an entire week, and this is not fun in the winter months, let me tell you.

At first, I was toughing it out, hopping in boot camp style, scrubbing, and getting my white butt out of there as fast as I could. Then, I tried the tactic of heating up water in the microwave, so I could at least wash my hair without getting hypothermia. Towards the end of my time, I actually dreaded the mornings because I knew I would have to do something unpleasant just to get ready for work. I started to get a little caught up in the situation and to feel a little bad for myself.

Isn't it funny how we can do that? Just a few months ago, I was in El Salvador, where conditions are not what we spoiled Americans are used to. I had to carry my own toilet paper in a backpack, and once used a cornfield as a bathroom. But fast-forward a little bit, and I am feeling sorry for myself that I have to take cold showers. In the grand scheme of things, a cold shower is a first world problem. And yet, it is so easy to have a first world problem consume your thoughts and make you feel like things are bad in life when, in fact, they are mostly really good. They cause us to complain and mope and lose track of all of our blessings.

Philippians 4:4 says, "Rejoice in the Lord always. I will say it again: Rejoice!" (NIV) Always is a tricky word, isn't it? But to rejoice at all times is not to say, "Hey God, thanks for this cold shower, which is freezing my hair into icicles." It is to find the good and thank Him for that. *Thank you that I have a home with running water.*

Thank you that I had the money in my account to get this fixed. Thank you for repairmen that come to my home. Thank you for being with me through troubles big and small.

Reflection:

What small troubles am I being a baby about? How can I find the good and thank God for it?

Day 68

The Israelites wandered in the desert for forty years, and they complained for 39.9 of it, it seems, when reading through their story. Sometimes, I read Bible stories and I think how frustrating the characters are. Leave them alone for a minute and they are fashioning a golden calf out of their earrings. Save them from slavery and they will complain about the food they have to eat. It's clear-cut to the reader how foolish and ungrateful they were in this process, but truth be told, we likely would have been the same way.

The story of the Israelites' escape from Egypt is remarkable. Moses convinces Pharaoh to let his people go, God parts the Red Sea, kills all their enemies, and provides day after day for his people. He sends a pillar of light so they can travel and see at night, he makes manna and then quail fall from the sky so they are nourished, and the Bible says that even though they walked and walked, their feet did not swell, and their clothes did not wear out for forty years.

Even so, they complain and complain and complain. When God's people finally reach the Promised Land, Moses gives them a little pep talk. He tells them they are about to embark on a wonderful new chapter, but warns them that they need to remember what God has done for them, so they don't become proud.

He says, "You may say to yourself, 'My power and the strength of my hands have produced this wealth for me.' But remember the Lord your God, for it is he who gives you the ability to produce wealth, and so confirms his covenant" (Deut. 8:18). Without God's provision, his people would have certainly died in that desert.

Enduring a deployment can be a little like wandering in the wilderness. There are times when it feels endless and frustrating. If you look back, though, you can identify the times when God's provision was clear. He provided daily manna through his word, his spirit, and his people when you were in a weary land. It is not our strength or tenacity that gets us through, but God's presence. Look back on this deployment and see if you can identify God's hand in different situations. How can you choose to be thankful for those times instead of complaining about the hardship?

Reflection:

How have I seen God provide for me during this deployment?

Temptation and Pride

Ever notice that the whisper of temptation can be
heard farther than the loudest cry to duty.

—Earl Wilson

Day 69

In one of the final scenes of his life on earth, Jesus tells Peter he will deny Christ three times. "Surely not," says Peter, "not even if I have to die!" Yet when Jesus is taken into custody, his disciples scatter. Jesus is taken to the high priest, and the gospels say that Peter "followed at a distance." Soon, he is being questioned by the people around him; and three times, Peter cries, "I don't know him! I am not with him!"

Do you notice the small steps in the progression of Peter denying Christ? He is a tenacious personality, and I have no doubt he loves Jesus. But see how following Jesus at a distance soon parlayed into Peter denying him altogether? Life is busy, and life with a husband deployed can feel downright chaotic, but the one thing we must find time for is communion with Christ. We must follow him closely, daily, so we will receive encouragement, wisdom, and guidance. The closer we keep to him, the easier it is to walk in his ways and become more like him. 1 Peter 2:21 says, "For this you have been called, because Christ suffered for you, leaving you an example, so that you might follow in his steps." Christ has called you to this life. Follow in his steps, and you will always be on the right path.

Reflection:

What is one way I can follow in Christ's steps? How will I stay close to Christ during this deployment?

Day 70

If you are a mom, you can relate to the feeling that no one is listening to you. You ask your child to clean his room, and it is still not done. You have to remind your kids over and over to brush their teeth, do their homework, and eat their vegetables. They know it all, or so they think, and they often tune us out, despite the fact that we know what is best for them, and care about their well being.

Jesus knew this feeling as well. He was God incarnate, but people still didn't want to hear his truth. They argued with him and tried to catch him doing something wrong. In a moment of utter sadness and disappointment, he stated of his people, "How often I have longed to gather your children together, as a hen gathers her chicks under her wings, and you were not willing" (Luke 13:34).

Jesus wants that none should perish, yet gives us free will to decide whether or not we will accept his gift. We are the scattered chicks, and Jesus longs to bring us near to him, and protect us, and we are too stubborn and oblivious to cooperate. I would like to think of myself as willing, but the truth is that there have been many times when I pushed Jesus away to take my own path. It happens when I put my desires first, when the words I choose are hurtful, and when I know what should be done, but chose not to do it.

I love the picture of Jesus gathering us together under his wings. It is so tender. It is protective. It is peaceful. Remind me why we wouldn't want to be there? Based on Jesus' statement, it seems like there are few qualifications to earn a spot there. Be willing. Be willing to rest, to cease striving, to trust him. Are you willing? Jesus waits.

Reflection:

How am I resisting Jesus from gathering me close to him?

Day 71

As I was leaving base recently, I couldn't help but notice a flashy little sports car in the lane next to me. It was silver, had a custom spoiler on the back, and custom rims. It had shiny chrome parts and had been totally tricked out. There was something else I couldn't help but notice, though. It sounded like a total piece of junk! This thing was loud as an airplane, and was being driven by someone who had no idea when to shift his manual transmission. It was painful to hear, really.

He pulled up beside me at the light to exit base, and we made eye contact. He revved up his engine to display his machismo, and I turned my head to watch the light. When it changed, we both gunned it, but I quickly took the lead, in my mini-van. That's right, I beat him off the block no sweat in my not-so-tricked-out Volkswagen mini-van. This thing is fueled by fruit snacks and cracker crumbs, and nothing else. After I was a good bit ahead of him, I changed lanes so I would be in front of him to rub it in. No one ever accused me of being mature.

Friends, we don't want to be a person who spends all their time making the outside look awesome when there is nothing of value inside. 1 Peter 3:3–4 says, "Your adornment must not be merely external—braiding the hair, and wearing gold jewelry, or putting on dresses; but let it be the hidden person of the heart, with the imperishable quality of a gentle and quiet spirit, which is precious in the sight of God."

I don't know about you, but gentle and quiet is not always how people describe me, but it's something I'm working on. Peter doesn't mean that we can't have a personality, or that we can't get dressed up and be girly. He means that we should find our strength and worth and beauty in Christ alone. What he finds beautiful is a woman who is resting and trusting in him.

Reflection:

What are some things that can be worked on from the inside?

Day 72

We all wear many hats, and can be like chameleons in our social lives. When we visit our child's school, we are the mom who has it all together. When we socialize with other military wives, we are well dressed with jewelry that coordinates and sassy heels. When we meet people, we are charming and kind; and when we're at church, we are friendly yet serious. We may change persona just walking from our minivan full of kids into the grocery store where there will be people watching and judging the behavior of our children. Psychologists would say this is normal. We learn as children to assess a situation and morph into someone who will fit in and keep the status quo. Most people want to feel accepted, and do not seek to continually rock the boat. Most people, that is, besides Jesus.

Many Christians have a mistaken concept of Jesus as meek, mild-mannered, or polite. *He sure was nice. I mean, he did good things for people, and he is the son of God, for Pete's sake.* This is true, but he was also a man who shouted at the Pharisees that they were a brood of vipers, and fashioned a whip to clear out the temple courts in righteous anger. When he was arrested, he stood before the religious and Roman leaders with few words. He did not even try to defend himself because he didn't owe anyone an explanation. When they asked if he was the Son of God, he simply said, "I AM." Jesus could have gone on a royal diatribe here. He could have stomped around and been like, "Man, my dad is going to be SO MAD when he hears about this!"

I am reminded of some celebrities who get arrested for something stupid, and they shout at the cops, "Do you know who I am?" Jesus would have been justified in this, but instead, he basically said, "Look, I am who I am. I don't owe you an explanation." He was so secure in himself, he would not deviate from his Father's plan one iota, and he was willing to be a boat-rocker because shaking things up would bring people to his kingdom.

Our desire to fit in and be liked is always going to be near the surface. We all like to be validated. However, we should not change to the point that we are not true to ourselves, or more importantly, to Christ. If we were held on trial, would there be enough evidence against us to prove we are followers of Christ? Do we feel the need to justify ourselves, or to become someone we are not so we don't rock the boat? Galatians 1:10 says, "For am I now seeking the approval of man, or of God? Or am I trying to please man? If I were still trying to please man, I would not be a servant of Christ" (ESV). Who are you trying to please?

Reflection:

Is there any place I go where I feel that I cannot be true to Christ?

Day 73

Years ago, my husband and I purchased a beautiful washer and dryer for our home. I say "beautiful" because the last set was a decade old, and caused us to put up with all kinds of nonsense. Sometimes, the washer wouldn't drain the water. Sometimes, the dryer wouldn't heat up at all. They were a lesson in patience and anger management. My husband is a planner, and he had researched every washer and dryer like it was his job. When he retires, he could rightfully have a position at Consumer Research Magazine, no doubt in my mind. He suggested we buy the pedestal that went under the washer and dryer. "You won't have to stoop that way," he suggested.

I looked only at the price tag, an extra $50 each. No way, we were already spending a small fortune on these things. I would be fine. My loving husband tried to reason with me, and I wasn't having it. Finally, he said, "Would you just let me do this for you?" Stubborn as I was, I insisted that, no, I would not. Do you see where this is going? He listened to me. After all, who is going to force someone to spend more money on something they insist they don't want? I think back on this conversation almost daily, as I complete loads of laundry while squatting to dig clothes out of the washer. Why didn't I just let him take care of me the way he wanted to? Why had I been so stubborn over something so silly?

Jesus described himself as a shepherd, someone who chooses to take care of naïve, helpless sheep (John 10). He gladly chooses this position. In Bible times, the shepherds were the lowest of low, not even allowed in the Temple. And Jesus, a king, chose this role to describe how he takes care of us. What a privilege for us, and yet, the parable where he uses this description of himself tells about how a sheep wandered away from him. He went after that sheep because he loved it and wished to take care of it and protect it. This is the picture of how he cares for us, if we will let him.

I won't lie, my stubbornness sometimes gets in the way of this, too. I make decisions without praying, and start to wander off a bit. Jesus wants us to be in close vicinity to him because he knows what is best, and desires the best for us. But he won't force us to stay. He doesn't build a fence around the sheep. It has to be a decision on our part to stay in eyesight of him.

Reflection:

How can I remain close to the Shepherd during this deployment?

Day 74

When my husband is home, I tend to be my best version of myself. I try to eat well, work out, keep the house clean, and have a decent meal on the table every night. When he's gone, I sometimes lose the ambition to do things the same way. Things start to slip a little. It becomes ordinary to run through a drive thru for dinner with the kids, let the dishes go, and wallow a little in self-pity. He is gone, so what is the point in it all? We have to be careful with the "I don't care attitude," because it is only a hop, skip, and a jump to living separate lives from our husbands that may include more toxic behaviors that could threaten our relationships.

It is when we are at a low that Satan attacks us the most. Think about the nature shows you've seen. The lion goes for the weakest prey it can find. If we have let our guard down, that is us! Without the accountability and company of our husbands around, we may slip back into bad behaviors. It is natural to do so, but let's remember that our nature is riddled with sinful desires. Things may seem like no big deal and balloon into something very bad if we're not careful. We each struggle with different vices, but when we are relying on something other than God to get us through our trials, it is unhealthy and quite possibly, sinful.

The Israelites were masters at turning away from God when they didn't feel his presence. Time and time again, he rescued them and provided for them, but they whined and complained and looked for excuses to do whatever felt good in the moment. At one point, they actually wanted to go back to Egypt where they were slaves because they were sick of their present conditions. Now, we can look at these stories and think, *they're crazy*. But the truth is, we do the same things in other ways. Proverbs 26:11 says, "As a dog returns to its vomit, so fools repeat their folly."

Sometimes, the Bible uses grossness to get a point across. It basically says that when we return to past sins, we are like a dog sucking up our vomit like it is crème brulee. It may be "innocently" making contact with an old boyfriend and acting flirtatiously. It may be drinking too much instead of taking our concerns to God. It could be nasty language, anger issues, binge eating, or hanging with the wrong crowd. Most of us are fully aware of what our issues are, and we must be vigilant to avoid our pitfalls.

Our husbands may be gone for an extended period of time, but the Lord of the Universe is on our speed dial. Don't cope in unhealthy or sinful ways. Take your concerns to him, and surround yourself with those who will love you and keep you honest. "Above all else, guard your heart, for everything you do flows from it" (Prov. 4:23).

Reflection:

Am I using something besides God to cope with my stress? Is this a healthy or unhealthy thing?

Day 75

Our society often throws around phrases like, "Follow your heart," and "Do what feels right to you," but what would the world look like if everyone took this stance? I am pretty much addicted to the show, *Hoarders*, which is ironic, considering its content. This show is drama-packed, and features individuals who have a compulsion to stuff their house full of things to the point of danger and disgusting conditions. They acquire more and more stuff, all at the peril of their relationships, health and sanity, and the thing that feels most unnatural and bad to them is getting rid of Cool Whip lids and used Ramen noodle cups.

ISIS members are likely "following their hearts." They believe Allah has given them authority to kill Christians, and they take their responsibility seriously, wreaking havoc on the entire Middle East, and showing no mercy even for the children they rape and behead.

I know these are extreme examples, but following your heart blindly can be dangerous. It relies on feelings, which are fickle. We see cute little hearts as decorations at Valentine's and on little girls' clothing, but what does the Bible says about our hearts? Jeremiah 17:9 says that it is deceitful above all things. Proverbs 4:23 tells us to guard our heart, because everything flows from it.

David was a man after God's heart (Acts 13:22). He loved the Lord, and wanted to do God's will. We should model ourselves after this. Following our feelings and our heart is giving in to our flesh, and we know that our flesh is at odds with our spirit (Gal. 5:17). We can easily buy into the trap that we deserve comfort while making this huge sacrifice. Maybe it is too many drinks, or the physical touch of someone who is not our husband. When something feels good and easy, we may need to hit the pause button and seek God's wisdom. It is when we seek His heart and not our own, that we are in His will.

Reflection:

What feels good and easy in my life? Is this a part of God's blessing, or a temptation?

Day 76

As a child, the story about Lot in Genesis 19 always amazed me, especially the part where his wife turned into a pillar of salt. As an adult, I examine this story and think what an excellent lesson it is for all of us. Lot was visited by angels of the Lord and told to get the heck out of Dodge. Fire and brimstone were on their way, and if they wanted to survive, they needed to beat it. Lot gathered up his family, and even though the ramifications were clear, the bible says *he hesitated.*

I read this story, and I wonder, why the heck is he hesitating? This is such a disgusting and depraved city. Lot sees the men of the town try to attack his angelic visitors just verses before, and by all implications, it is a terrible and dangerous place to be, yet he hesitates. Sodom was what he knew, and he wasn't going to let go of it yet, no matter how bad it was. Thankfully, because of God's mercy, the angels yanked him out of town and saved his life. His family is told to run for it, and whatever you do, don't look back, but Lot's wife couldn't let go. She still yearned for her comfort zone. As disgusting as Sodom was, she just couldn't let go. She broke the angel's command and was turned to salt.

Is there something you're having a hard time letting go of? Unhealthy things, especially sinful things, can get ahold of us, and even though we know intellectually that they are toxic, we keep returning to them. We keep turning around to them. Thankfully, 2 Corinthians 5:17 tells us that, "Therefore, if anyone is in Christ, the new creation has come. The old has gone, the new is here!" We don't have to turn back to the things that are hurting us. We are a new creation in Christ, and we can walk forward by his grace.

Reflection:

What temptation or unhealthy thing am I holding on to? How can I give it up to God?

Day 77

I will never forget the feeling I had upon seeing the Atlantic Ocean for the first time as a child. It seemed endless. I felt so small. I looked at the expanse of sand, stretching for miles. It occurred to me that God knew the number of grains of sand on that beach. He knows the number of stars in the sky and hairs on your head. But he is not just a God of mass quantity. He is so big and knowing that every part of his creation is intimate to him.

When we become too big in our own estimation, we begin to think we can do it all on our own. We spin our wheels, try to manipulate every situation, and go into problem-solving mode, instead of relying on God and his perfect will in our lives. Picture the planet earth. Now picture how big our galaxy, the Milky Way, is. Did you know there are distant stars bigger than our entire galaxy? What does that say about our God? How big and powerful is the God who made all these things? I can't even fathom.

Yet, Christ humbled himself (Phil 2:8) when he came to earth as a helpless babe. The creator of the world had to learn to walk, talk, and had to depend completely on someone else to even stay alive. If he can be humble, how much more so should we!

Why do I think I know better? Why would I go one day without consulting him on what his will is for me, for each and every day? I am a speck on a planet that is a speck in a galaxy that is not even a speck in God's enormous creation. Can I rely on the God that knows me so intimately to do what is best for me? Can I yield my will to his and say without question, thy will be done, Lord?

Reflection:

How am I limiting God in my life? How big will I let him be?

Day 78

Being away from your husband for long periods of time is challenging in many ways, but a big one is missing his affection. At the end of a long, hard day it is difficult to go to bed alone. You long to have someone wrap their arms around you and hold you. You desire intimacy. You feel lonely. All these feelings are normal when you haven't seen your husband in months. One reassurance we have is the verse that says we have no temptation that isn't common to man (1 Cor. 10:13). As far as we know, Jesus relied only on the companionship of his friends to get him through his life, and he had so many stressors and hardships. Still, he was a man with human desires and did not sin.

Being alone is hard, and temptation will come knocking on our door. It is when we are at our lowest that Satan brings the sneakiest attacks. We may feel justified or even a little angry with our husbands for making us live this way. We may be at a low point where we crave attention so much we choose to do something we wouldn't normally do. We each know our pitfalls; and if we're honest, we know when we're flirting with danger. When that little voice inside us speaks up, we should not ignore it. When we have that feeling that something is wrong, we should heed it. This can be manifested in many ways— not accepting a friend request from an old boyfriend, not returning an email that could open a door to a dangerous situation, or avoiding any situation that could cause temptation, like going to a club or bar. We each know our weaknesses and should not put ourselves in situations that would compromise us.

Just as our husbands guard themselves for their work, we need to guard our hearts carefully in their absence. Proverbs 4:23 says, "Guard your heart above all else, for it determines the course of your life."

Reflection:

What will the course of your life be? What decisions can you make today to be on God's path and not your own?

Day 79

Being alone is not easy. God designed marriage to be a husband and wife "cleaving" to one another. In other words, we are supposed to be close. This is not always possible in the military life, as you well know. When Jesus went into the wilderness and was tempted, he was all alone, too, and this is when the Devil attacked him relentlessly. Satan appealed to every weakness a human has, trying to trip him up and ruin him for his mission ahead of being a blameless, spotless sacrifice for us. If Jesus had given in, his purpose in coming to earth would have been destroyed, but he knew the stakes.

It is easy to read the stories of Jesus and picture him as a Bible-times Superman, minus the cape. He performs miracles, is perfect in every way, and is everything we wish we could be. It is so important to remember that Jesus is not just fully God, but fully man as well. He isn't using tricks when he is being tempted in the wilderness. He is tapping into the power of God to resist the temptation. Guess what? We can do the same.

So much of avoiding temptation is avoiding what leads up to it. We know our pressure points and our weaknesses. If there is a man that is making you think about things you shouldn't, stay away from him. If there is a person who is emotionally taking the place of your husband, distance yourself from them. If there is someone to whom you bad-mouth or disparage your husband, stop talking to them in that way. Your husband alone deserves your heart, and that means physically and emotionally. An affair is sharing yourself in any way that is reserved for your husband. We need to be faithful to them in every way.

We are not alone when temptation comes, and you can believe that it will. Hebrews 2:18 tells us that, because Jesus himself suffered when he was tempted, "he is able to help those who are being tempted." Ask for his help to resist temptation, and ask that God will make our hearts soft to his reproach when we are starting to cross the line into something inappropriate in our relationships.

Reflection:

What line am I flirting with currently? What situation do I need to step away from?

Day 80

I am one of those people who has loads of patience in the big things, but little patience in small, annoying situations. I may possibly lose my mind when someone is clicking a pen, and please do not take up the entire grocery aisle with your cart while deciding which yogurt has more calories. It is something God is still trying to work out in me, and may take me until my deathbed. Even there, I will likely be impatient.

It was like this one day when I was driving on a busy road and a driver cut in front of me and left their turn signal on. Bad drivers make me especially frustrated. Ain't nobody got time for that! He insistently drove down the road with that turn signal on, slowly driving me crazy. He even switched it, left to right, before speeding off like a crazy person. It wasn't until I got to an intersection when my engine quieted and I heard the blink, blink, blink of my own turn signal. It appeared that I had been driving that whole time with it flashing! In fact, it slowly registered that this was why that man had pulled in front of me flashing his turn signals, because he was trying to give me a clue! I had been so focused on him that I didn't realize I was the screw-up!

It is easy to observe others and see glaring faults. They are all around us. We sometimes even dismiss people because the bad is all we are able to see. Matthew 7:1–5 says, "Do not judge, or you too will be judged. For in the same way you judge others, you will be judged, and with the measure you use, it will be measured to you. Why do you look at the speck of sawdust in your brother's eye and pay no attention to the plank in your own eye? How can you say to your brother, 'Let me take the speck out of your eye,' when all the time there is a plank in your own eye? You hypocrite, first take the plank out of your own eye, and then you will see clearly to remove the speck from your brother's eye." Ouch. When I focus on other's problems, I am overlooking my own.

Reflection:

What in my life needs to be examined? How much time do I spend being critical, and how can I curb this habit?

Day 81

Have you ever heard of the 80/20 Rule? It is the idea that infidelity in a marriage occurs because we feel we are missing something in our relationship. Your marriage may be 80% good, but you tend to dwell on the 20% that lacks. Some people over-compensate for this by searching for that 20% in someone else, however, they are only that 20%, and are lacking the substance of the 80% you have at home. An example would be a woman who is frustrated with her husband for not being attentive to her and cheats on him with someone who makes her feel special only to find out that this man doesn't like kids, doesn't have a job, and chews with his mouth open. By the time she figures this out, she has imploded her marriage and life.

The 80/20 Rule can definitely be viewed in its natural habitat as the time wears on and men and women suffer from loneliness and lack of physical contact. One may even feel just a smidge bit justified in their actions because of the hardship faced in a deployment. Maybe there were even unresolved problems in the marriage before he left, and they are exacerbated in this trying time. Mathematically, it doesn't make sense, but it can be tempting to trade in the 80% for 20% of companionship or just plain sex when you are missing your spouse. You may even convince yourself that no one would be the wiser. Isaiah 47:10 says, "You have trusted in your wickedness and have said, 'No one sees me.' Your wisdom and knowledge mislead you when you say to yourself, 'I am, and there is none besides me'" (NIV).

The Message version of the Bible says it best with, "There's more to sex than mere skin on skin. Sex is as much spiritual mystery as physical fact. As written in Scripture, "The two become one." Since we want to become spiritually one with the Master, we must not pursue the kind of sex that avoids commitment and intimacy, leaving us more lonely than ever—the kind of sex that can never "become one." There is a sense in which sexual sins are different from all others. In sexual sin, we violate the sacredness of our own bodies, these bodies that were made for God-given and God-modeled love, for "becoming one" with another. Or didn't you realize that your body is a sacred place, the place of the Holy Spirit?" (1 Cor. 6:8). Don't chase after the 20%. Guard your body and your marriage. Look for means to connect with your husband that are intimate in other ways.

Reflection:

Do I find myself daydreaming about what it would be like to be with someone else? How could this be dangerous?

Waiting

Our willingness to wait reveals the value we
place on what we're waiting for.

–Charles Stanley

Day 82

As military wives, we are used to the idea of waiting. We wait
for calls, letters, appointments, test results, due dates, and homecomings. We learn to occupy ourselves with other things in the meantime, and carry on with our lives and responsibilities. Fussing and
worrying will not make the date come any faster. Do we wait on God
like this? Many of us pray for concerns, or ask for God's guidance on
a matter, and then want the response yesterday. In our world of modern conveniences, we get used to not having to wait for anything. We
can heat up a meal in a couple of minutes and fast forward through
TV commercials on our DVR. We can get so impatient when God
doesn't text us right back with an answer.

The bible says we must wait on the Lord, and I don't think that
means in the pacing, sighing, sulking way. His ways are not our ways,
and his time is not our time. He has everything worked out on his
time frame, and trust me, it's for the best. If you put the Thanksgiving
turkey in the oven to roast for the big dinner, grew impatient, and
took it out after twenty minutes, what would be the result? Likewise,
God is grooming us, refining us, and preparing us for the things that
happen in our lives. Psalm 27:13–14 says, "Yet I am confident I will
see the Lord's goodness while I am here in the land of the living. Wait
patiently for the Lord. Be brave and courageous. Yes, wait patiently

for the Lord." We need to trust in his timing, and wait diligently and patiently, because he's got it all figured out.

Reflection:

What am I growing impatient about, and how can I trust that it will unfold in God's timing?

Day 83

When there is a special occasion at our house and the oldest gets to pick what is for dinner, he inevitably picks crab legs, which is a hit with everyone. Crab legs are a messy and pain-staking meal to eat, and they require a lot of patience and know-how. You have to know which joint to start at, how to crack the leg just so, and then pull the meat oh-so-gently out of its casing. The payoff is fantastic—buttery, soft, and juicy goodness that melts in your mouth. It's a lot of work eating crab, and every time I do, I wonder who the first person was that looked at this glorified bug and thought it would be a tasty treat.

There are things in life that people pass up on because they require "too much" work. My dad would be the first to say that he doesn't have the patience for crab legs, and sort of thinks all the cracking is gross. That is fine. More for me. But seriously, there are many important things that people don't experience because they seem too hard on the surface. It may be a goal that seems too lofty, such as going back to college or running a half-marathon. It may even be the energy that is required to make a relationship work while a husband is deployed.

Being a military wife is not for the faint of heart. We may send letters and packages, thoughtful gifts, and encouraging emails just for one nugget of feeling normal with our spouse. Just like the crab legs, it takes a lot of work for a little payoff, but anything worth having is worth working for. "Commit to the Lord everything you do, and he will establish your plans" (Prov. 16:3).

Reflection:

What seems too hard in my life right now? How can I commit this situation to the Lord? How will this period of waiting pay off in my relationship?

Day 84

My son's bus is incredibly unpredictable. Hudson will rush out to the stop, wanting to be on time, and wait. And wait. And wait. He is patient for a while, but soon, he is pacing and checking his Lego watch. Where is the bus? It was supposed to be here by now! One day, he waited a very long time and finally gave up. He trudged back home, disappointed. He reported the news, the bus was not coming. As he finished his explanation, you can guess what drove by—the bus! After all that waiting, he didn't hold out long enough to make it.

We can be like this in our lives. God has promised us blessings if we are willing to wait. Sarah waited about ninety years to have her son, Isaac. Ruth waited through the death of her husband, a move to a foreign land, and years of hard labor. If you are waiting for God to come through for you, you are in good company. Psalm 130:5 says, "I wait for the Lord, my soul waits, and in his word I hope." You don't need to pace, sigh or nag God. He will come through when his timing is right. Don't give up just to see that bus drive by! What would have happened if Sarah and Ruth had given up? These were women chosen to be in the lineage of Christ. They were steadfast, and he used that to bring Salvation into the world.

Reflection:

What good may come of my waiting? How is God making this time of waiting purposeful in the story of my life?

Day 85

Some nights, when it storms, there will be a little knock at my bedroom door. Even at nine years old, there are times when my biggest boy just needs his mommy and daddy. He is way too big to get in bed with us, but he knows the policy that he can bring his pillow and blanket and set up a little bed next to ours. Just this proximity gives him confidence to know that he is safe and taken care-of.

I find that it is the same with my relationship to Jesus. Times get hard or scary, and I just want to be near him. Last month, I found a lump on my breast, and try as I might to put it out of my mind, I was very, very nervous waiting for results of the biopsy. When the results came back, they were inconclusive. My doctor wished to do a more invasive biopsy and the wait started again. It was grueling, but in that time, I drew near to Christ, and I felt his presence with me as I prayed and searched his word for comfort.

The results came back negative, and I must confess, after a period of thankfulness, my devotion to our quiet time started slipping. During the time of waiting, I sought him all day long every time a nervous bubble of anxiety popped into my stomach. After I received the good news, I am ashamed to say I took a step back. Waiting is hard, and worrying can bring us closer to Jesus. We must be careful to not withdraw when the wait is over, or we feel like the storm has passed. "Be still before the Lord and wait patiently for him" (Ps. 37:7, NIV).

Reflection:

Why do I have a relationship with Jesus? Is it to be saved from consequences, or do I crave his presence in the everyday and mundane?

Day 86

When I was a child, I would ask my mom for things, and oftentimes, she would reply with, "We'll see." I'll be honest—it would infuriate me. As kids (and sometimes even adults) we feel such an urgency to get what we want. We need it right away. I saw my mom as the person that could make that happen at the snap of her fingers. So why was she holding out on me? Looking back, I can see that sometimes, when my mom gave the "we'll see" response, it was because she had something waiting in the wings. For example, I would ask for a toy and she knew that she had already purchased it for my birthday. In her case, "we'll see" meant "wait." As an immature kid, I thought her response meant no, but she was really saying, "Just wait a bit until the timing is right."

God does the same with us. Someone once told me God answers prayers with yes, no, and not right now. The problem is, we want everything RIGHT NOW. Our lives have gotten so convenient with modern technology that we are not used to waiting for much. The people of the Bible knew how to wait because they were used to it. If they were hungry, they would hunt for fruits, vegetables, or animals. If they needed to cook, they would search firewood for a fire that they made without a barbeque grill. They would pluck, butcher, clean, and forge metal for pots and pans. If I am hungry on the go, I swing through a Chick-fil-A drive thru and I'm done. Psalm 27:14 says, "Wait for the Lord; Be strong and let your heart take courage; Yes, wait for the Lord." He says it twice, so you know it's important! If you ask for something and feel like you are not getting the answer you wanted, take heart. God is not holding out on you. He has devised a plan that is perfect for you if you will just wait.

Reflection:

To what is God saying, "not right now" to me? How can I wait patiently to see God's plan unfold?

Day 87

If you have ever been around children leading up to Christmastime, you know how impatient they can be. This past Christmas, my four-year-old asked me on a daily basis, "Is Christmas tomorrow, Mama?" I would shake my head and smile. He was so earnest, and had no concept of time. He just knew that it was coming and was going to be the most amazing day of presents, food and family.

I can't imagine what the people of the Old Testament must have felt when they heard God's word delivered from the prophets. A Messiah was coming, one who would solve all their problems, and rule forever. These prophets began foretelling the coming of Christ hundreds of years before it would come to pass, and my kid thought he had a long time to wait! When Christ did finally make his appearance, it was an unexpected one. The Savior would come as a child, born to average people in a barn. He would not be the political leader they were expecting, but would give healing to those he encountered, and life to those who believed.

Christ promises that, one day, we will have a place with him in Heaven if we believe in him. He will return for us at the perfect time, and take us home to be with him. Although he has made this clear, I don't think we always live our lives as if we have this hope. We get bogged down by little things, lose hope in the situation we are in, and lose sight of the amazing promise we have been given. We even live our lives bound by sin that God gives us the strength to overcome. Jesus came to offer us life, and abundantly so. If we focus on him, we can have it. "But our citizenship is in heaven. And we eagerly await a Savior from there, the Lord Jesus Christ, who, by the power that enables him to bring everything under his control, will transform our lowly bodies so that they will be like his glorious body" (Phil. 3:20).

Reflection:

Am I living my life like a child of God? Do I look at things with an eternal perspective?

Communication

Communication works for those who work at it.

-John Powell

Day 88

One night, as I tucked my eight-year-old into bed, he looked up at me and said, "Mom, why doesn't God just talk to us? I mean, if he's really there, why can't we see him? He could just tell us what to do." I must confess, I was caught off-guard. Most of our bedtime discussions involve recapping the day's activities or sheepishly telling me about the girl he likes in his third grade class. But this was different, and let's be honest, something we have all wondered at one time or another. In the midst of trials, we sometimes feel God's presence intensely. Other times, we are left wondering, *God where are you?*

The Israelites experienced this frequently as they went through trial after trial, including being held captive by the Egyptians. The Bible tells us they cried out to the Lord, and he heard them. He made a way for them to break free from Pharaoh, and he provided for them daily with manna, but they grappled with the fact that they couldn't see their God. The Egyptians had gods made of gold that everyone could see; and no matter how the one true God made a way for the Israelites, they weren't satisfied. In fact, when Moses went to commune with the Lord on a mountain to receive his law, the Israelites went so far as to make a golden calf that they worshipped in place of God, giving thanks that the calf brought them out of Egypt. They were so fickle and impatient that they refused to see that God was all around them.

137

As the Israelites traveled, God appeared as a cloud by day and a pillar of fire by night so he would guide the way they should take (Neh. 9:12). No matter how they rebelled, they were his people, and he would lead them. Today, we have God's word as a way to know his character and ways for our life. Psalm 119:105 says that his word is a lamp unto our feet, and a light unto our path. It is not a horoscope that tells us daily what to expect, but a guide book that shows us the overall big picture of what God wants of us: humility, respect, and love toward others. God also gave us the Holy Spirit who speaks quietly in our hearts. There will be days when we feel like God is far away, busy or uncaring, but this is far from the truth. When we cry out to him, he hears us. He may not send us a text, but his Word endures, and will remind us of his faithfulness, no matter the circumstance. Quiet your heart, and he will speak to you. The next time you feel, *God where are you?* Remember Hebrews 13:5, "I will never leave you nor forsake you." He is close, my friend.

Reflection:

Does God feel close or far away right now? What may be the reason for this feeling?

Day 89

When Brett and I first started dating, it was puppy love. We were pathetic. I thought about him day and night, and when we couldn't be together, it felt like torture. He would make romantic gestures, both big and small, to express his love to me. Once, he had to go away for a few weeks, and he would send me love letters, one of which said, "I (Heart) Mackenzie C." in huge letters. He was constantly pursuing me in an effort to show me his feelings for me.

Fast forward fifteen years, and the picture is slightly different. Of course, our love is strong, but it is completely different, as we feel we don't have as much to prove to one another. He knows that I know that he loves me, and while there are still romantic gestures, he is not constantly trying to put on the hard press. When we are at home together, we are dressed in sweats, and if we feel a fart come on, we just let it rip. (Don't judge, you know you do it!) Our relationship has become comfortable.

God is not the same. He is in constant pursuit of us, and is always expressing his love to us. "How precious are your thoughts about me, O God. They cannot be numbered! I can't even count them; they outnumber the grains of sand! And when I wake up, you are still with me!" (Pss. 139:17–18). The Bible is filled with stories of God loving and pursuing his people, even when they pushed him away, ran away, or tried to do things on their own. God never gives up on us. His love letters for us are written all over our lives. They are the gift of our husband, our children, our friends, our family, nature, the stars, and our beloved pets; basically anything that brings us joy. His love is constant and passionate for us, year after year.

Reflection:

How can I reciprocate God's love for me? What is it God desires in return from me?

Day 90

My grandparents were foundational in my beliefs and the older I get, I look back and realize what an impact they had on my life. They were involved by talking with me, attending my school events, and hosting family gatherings, but what has left the biggest impression on me is how they prayed. They took prayer very seriously, and it wasn't until I saw it in person that I could fully understand. They would pray for hours on end, passionately interceding on behalf of every single person in the family, missionaries, our nation's leaders, and more. Even when they were well into their elderly years, they would arrive early to church and get on their knees before the service. Now as an adult, I cherish those memories of their care and concern for others. Who knows how their prayers impacted my life. They asked God for my safety and success each and every night of my life. I am most likely blessed today because of the prayers they covered me with as a child.

Prayer is so important as it is a connection to God, but it is also an exercise in humbling yourself and turning over your thoughts and worries to the one who made you. Prayer is also a gift you can give someone. Who is praying for your husband and children? You may be blessed to have other godly people in your family lifting them up, but you may also be the only one. We tuck our babies in with care, make sure their lunch is packed just right, and wash and fold uniforms, but the best way we can care for our loved ones is to pray for them. It is also the best way to receive peace in your own life, especially during stressful deployments.

Then they cried to the LORD in their trouble,
and he delivered them from their distress. He

made the storm be still, and the waves of the sea were hushed. Then they were glad that the waters were quiet, and he brought them to their desired haven. (Ps. 107:28–30)

Reflection:

How seriously do I take the privilege and responsibility of prayer?

Day 91

In the Garden of Eden, man and woman are tempted by what they think they don't have. God has given them everything they need, but when the serpent makes them believe God is holding out on them, they cash it all in for a mirage. Eve was the first to eat the fruit, and then she gives her seal of approval, handing it to Adam, who eats as well. For certain, Adam made his own decision, and should have been a better leader, but Eve was the one who handed it to him, suggesting that it was good, and he took it.

This story presents an interesting picture on the dynamics of a marriage. The Bible says that the husband is to be the head of the home, the leader, but there is no doubt how influential a wife is. She is the heart of the relationship, and the husband listens to her advice and trusts her judgment.

What are we "offering" our husbands? We need to be diligent in what we are feeding them, and I'm not talking about casseroles here! While they are gone, our husbands need encouragement and reassurance. On deployments, there is often infrequent communication. How are we using our time? Are we complaining, or are we reassuring him that we support him and we're proud of him? Are we building him up, or criticizing him? In the case of Adam and Eve, their choice altered their lives dramatically, and the future of the whole world. Transversely, our support can encourage and strengthen our men. Proverbs 15:4 says that, "The tongue that brings healing is a tree of life." How will you use your words to help your husband?

Reflection:

What is the nature of the way I talk to my husband? How can I improve on the way I communicate with him?

Day 92

In the military, the ranks work on a "need to know" basis. The lowest man on the totem pole is only told the bare minimum and is not privy to much information. As you work your way up the ranks, you start to get the inside scoop. Everyone has a boss above them until you get to the top, the Commander in Chief. The President of the United States has the highest clearance, and he knows everything there is to know. All intelligence, recon, and research are reported to him.

In life, we feel like we should always be in the know. We are impatient when we don't understand something, and we demand answers of God. We want to know why He let something happen, or what the future holds for us. We want answers. Here's the trouble, we are not in the "need to know." God has arranged things for a purpose. We are not given all the information, and this makes us depend on Him for wisdom and guidance. The truth is, if we knew all the answers up front, we would probably screw it all up or be completely overwhelmed. We would depend on our own strength instead of His.

There is good reason for having ranks and keeping certain information private from most people. In our case, our Lord of Lords is a trustworthy king who has our very best interest at heart. In times when we don't understand something, we can trust that he is working everything out for his glory. "Trust in the Lord with all your heart, and lean not unto your own understanding. In all your ways, acknowledge him, and he will direct your paths" (Prov. 3:5–6).

Reflection:

What unknowns do I struggle with the most? What are some ways God has worked out the unknowns in the past?

Day 93

Jesus told stories with examples the people of the time would understand. He spoke of bread, wine, hard work, and fishing. These were examples the people could wrap their heads around. When Jesus spoke about yeast, everyone knew what he was talking about because bread was a staple of daily life. In Matthew 16, Jesus warns his disciples to beware the yeast of the Pharisees. He goes on to explain that even the smallest amount of yeast gets mixed in to a batch of dough and changes the entire composition of it.

Recently, I have been trying my hand at making homemade bread, and I can tell you this is true. When I mix up my dough, it looks normal, but after I let it sit, it puffs up and over the top of my bowl. If you've ever eaten flatbread, you know what a difference a yeast makes. In bread, this is a good thing, but in Jesus' example, he used yeast to describe a bad thing—the Pharisees who pretended to be righteous, but did not love the Lord and stirred up dissention among those who were around Christ.

I also think about how our words can be like yeast, which mixes through the entire batch of someone's life. What kind of words are we using? When we talk with our husband, are we resentful? Are we building him up and encouraging him? How do we speak to our children? Are we impatient and snappy? What are the words we use with our friends and family? Are we critical or gossipy? The words we use have the ability to build someone up or cut them down, and like yeast, permeate to the deepest part of a person. Challenge yourself to use only words that encourage and edify today.

Reflection:

What are ways in which I can encourage someone with my words today?

Day 94

When my husband is deployed, communication is pretty bad. He is on a ship, and so far, they do not have the technology to video chat, which has become common in other branches. We email, instant message, and talk very infrequently. Sometimes, we'll be talking on the phone and get cut off mid-sentence. Sometimes, emails go unanswered or they are misunderstood. Sometimes, they are in a dangerous situation and turn off all communication, and you can't talk for days or weeks.

Talking to God can be a little of the same. Sometimes, we feel like our communication with him is spotty. We may feel like He's not hearing us, or we haven't heard from him in a while. Sometimes, we feel like he's ignoring what we're saying. Maybe we have a bad connection through no fault but our own.

In the Old Testament, God often spoke directly to his people giving them directives. In modern day, this rarely happens. We are not left alone, however. We have his Spirit to guide us, prayer, his holy word, and even other Christians to speak his truth to us.

Psalm 119:105 says that God's word is a lamp unto our feet and a light unto our path. If we focus on him and what has been written, his desire for our lives and even just our day to day will become more evident.

Reflection:

How can I improve communication with God on my end?

Day 95

When I was in sixth grade I owned a Golden Retriever named Sherlock who was my world. He was always by my side and loved to take up most of my twin bed at night, especially when he was scared by a thunderstorm. One Christmas, my mom bought me a sweatshirt with a picture of a Golden retriever that looked just like Sherlock, and I couldn't wait to wear it to school. I was just so proud. Then it happened. The day came for me to return after winter break, and I walked into school feeling good. That is until I sat in my assigned seat next to Ryan, a smug boy who gave me a hard time pretty much every day. He took one look at my beloved shirt and said, "You are what you wear!" It took me a second to realize he was calling me a dog, the most common insult of the day. He thought I was ugly. I couldn't get home fast enough that day to tear off that shirt and plunge it to the bottom of my dresser drawer, never to be worn again.

Words hurt. I am now in my thirties, and while I am not pained by Ryan's words anymore, I still remember them. I have a friend who thinks of a punk kid's words every time she gets her hair cut because he told her that her hair was the only good thing about her. I bet you have a similar story. Obviously, adolescence is a vulnerable period of time for our emotions, but our words have a lot of power. James describes our words as sparks that can start a fire, or the rudder of a ship that steers the whole vessel (James 3:6). In Galatians, Paul describes how a little yeast stirs into an entire batch of bread when admonishing Christians for being led astray by words. Our words can give life or serve to discourage. Once they are released from our lips, we don't have the ability to take them back or change the way they make someone feel about themselves. That is why we need to take the utmost care that we are speaking life into our husbands, children, friends and family. Ephesians 4:29 reminds us, "Do not let any unwholesome talk come out of your mouths, but only what is helpful for building others up according to their needs, that it may benefit those who listen."

Reflection:

How can I use my words in a powerfully positive way today? What genuine compliments can I offer the people around me?

Day 96

Have you ever been really excited about something, and had someone close to you completely shut you down? After I had my second baby, I decided something drastic was in order to lose the extra pounds. I was not even someone who jogged, but I signed up for a half-marathon at my husband's encouragement. I figured, if I didn't want to die, I would have to train, and training would get me back into shape. I was really excited and motivated. I had a vision.

That's when they came out, the "boo birds"— people who were discouraging to my goal. Instead of just seeing my training as something that was not for everyone, they criticized me because it wasn't for them. "Isn't that a lot of time away from your children to train? I could never drop my child off with someone at the gym," or "Are you sure you're going to finish? Thirteen miles is a long way!"

I was already not getting enough sleep and on edge. Mix in some health troubles, and I was at my breaking point. I felt like no one understood me, and worse yet, some women around me just wanted to take me down a notch.

Being catty and discouraging is common, but social media has made it so much easier. Something someone would never say to your face is typed onto your profile with no second thought. People think they can say whatever they want if they follow it with a smiley face, or the annoying phrase, "Just saying." We can't stop people from being like this. In fact, we should probably work on growing thicker skin so people aren't constantly hurting our feelings. More importantly, though, we should make sure we're not the ones bursting others' bubbles.

What does it take to say a kind word instead of a critical one? There is no more energy involved. Cattiness is in most women's nature, I believe. We are competitive and jealous creatures if we don't control ourselves. 1 Thessalonians 5:11 tells us to build one another up and encourage one another. Words have life. They can encourage someone, but also chop them off at the knees. Choose wisely what you say, and lay down your own pride so you can speak life into someone.

Reflection:

Is there someone in my life I have the tendency to be catty with? What is it about them that threatens me?

Day 97

We lived in Rhode Island for two years while my husband attended the Naval War College, and it was two of the best years of his career, in my opinion. Summers were beyond compare. They were filled with beach time, boating, lobster bisque, and beautiful sunsets. Winters, well, that is a whole other subject. You see, in Rhode Island, they get snow. I don't mean your aww-that's-pretty type of snow. I mean two-feet-overnight-power-is-out snow. On one occasion, our power was out for days, and our house got down to 45 degrees. I actually had our children sleeping in their snowsuits. We had no outside contact, no TV, no cell phone coverage, and no internet. We were like Laura Ingalls, for Pete's sake. The only way to get a hot meal was to shovel a path to our gas grill and stand outside in hurricane force winds.

Being shut off from the world taught me two things. One is that I rely on TV way too much to entertain my kids. The other is that silence and stillness actually made me uncomfortable. My life is go, go, go. I am multi-tasking almost every minute of my day. I check my email while watching TV while having a conversation with my husband. I know you can relate. On those days, when it was silent in my house (except for boys whining that they were still unable to watch Sponge Bob), I learned what true stillness actually is, and how overtaken my little world is with filler. The TV is blaring, I am on my cell phone, and have the radio playing songs for good measure. Y'all, we sometimes have a few TVs on *at once* in the house. How am I supposed to hear God in all that mess?

Psalm 46:10 says, "Be still and know that I am God," and 1 Kings 19:12 describes God's voice as a "gentle whisper." Can I really hear God's voice in the midst of all these distractions? Our lives are busy, probably too busy, and in the advent of modern conveniences, we are now cramming a ridiculous amount of stuff into our days. Ironically, we also find ourselves asking, "Why doesn't God speak to me? Why does God feel so far away?" Maybe we should be asking ourselves if we are even listening. Why do we fool ourselves into believing more is better? More is just more, and it hampers our ability to listen to that still, small voice of God. He will not compete for our attention or shout over our TV. We must find that silent place to meet him and honor him with our undivided attention.

Reflection:

Am I taking quiet time to listen to God? If not, when can I carve out some time, and make it a part of my routine?

Day 98

I work with a non-profit organization that rescues local women who have been trapped in the sex trafficking industry. We sometimes get calls for immediate help from women who are trying to get away. Once, a woman was so desperate to escape her pimp, she ran away in her socks. We picked her up, got her medical care, and arranged for a local shelter to take her in. She was afraid for her life and afraid her pimp would find her and beat her up like the last time she tried to escape. The women who were helping her at the time were with her at the shelter, trying to get her checked in when the shelter staff stated that she would not be able to keep her cell phone while she stayed there. This was a deal breaker for our girl, and she opted to leave the shelter and fend for herself elsewhere.

This story may seem unbelievable, and may have even upset you a little. She wouldn't stay in a safe place because she had to give up her cell phone? From the outside, we can see that the shelter is the best choice, and she is likely in danger anywhere else, but to her, the shelter was unknown and uncomfortable. As terrible as things were in her life, she knew what to expect. She would rather be in a dangerous place than give up her security blanket. We respected her decision and dropped her off with a friend, not knowing how things would end for her. We are much the same in our relationship with Christ. Notice all the actions that must be done on our part. *Seek* and you will find. *Ask* and you shall receive. In Revelation 3:20, Jesus says, "Here I am! I stand at the door and knock. If anyone hears my voice and opens the door, I will come in and eat with that person, and they with me." Notice how it doesn't portray Jesus as some firefighter who busts down the door with an axe and sweeps us over his shoulder to safety. It is something we must choose and something we must respond to because he will never force our hand. He wants our love, not robotics.

What change are you fighting? What has that still, quiet voice told you that needs to be addressed? Jesus is not going to force you to fix it, but can you trust that he has the best choice for you? He is not trying to be a buzz kill. He is quietly knocking, hoping you will do what is best.

Reflection:

Has there been a time when I have accepted Jesus Christ to lead my life? If not, what is holding me back?

Day 99

I love politics, but I hate politics. Makes perfect sense, right? Politics stirs something up in me, and brings a passion to life that I have for few other things. Reading or watching a news story can make my heart and mind race, and I have opinions I just want to shout from the rooftops. Unfortunately, this sort of behavior does not exactly foster friendship in life. Politics in our country reaches a fever pitch during election cycles, and you can expect to see a zillion commercials, get robo-calls from candidates, and see Facebook friends argue non-stop about issues.

When my husband's command goes to sea, those who stay behind are constantly reminded of OPSEC, or Operational Security. Loose lips sink ships and all that. There are very strict guidelines about what can and can't be said to others about where our spouses are, what they are doing, etc. You can't sneeze without the ombudsman using "that tone" to warn you how crucial it is to observe OPSEC. As annoying as it can be when someone takes OPSEC to the nth degree, it is necessary to protect our guys.

I wish we had some sort of a civilian version of OPSEC for politics on Facebook (possibly FACESEC? POLITICSEC? MOUTHSEC? We need to work on this.). I have learned that you cannot debate politics on Facebook no matter how genuine or respectful you think you can be. It always blows up in your face, especially if it is a topic of passion for you. Try as you might, you cannot argue about abortion or gun ownership without losing a few friends. You may not even engage in debate, but just post a bunch of memes making fun of a politician; and trust me, you will lose the respect of many people. Don't believe me? Just think of someone from your own page who drives you nuts with posts that are obnoxious. We all have one or seventy-eight.

Romans 12:18 says, "If it is possible, as far as it depends on you, live at peace with everyone."

Now, for some people, it just won't be possible to live at peace. There are those who live to cause strife, and you may have to set up some healthy boundaries. (Too bad there isn't an "Unfollow" button in life! I'm kidding…maybe.) That "as far as it depends on you" is the sticky part of the sentence, though. If I'm honest, there's a lot I can do to keep the peace, including not posting certain things, and not being baited into commenting on things that pluck my nerves. Emotions run high when we are missing someone we love. We may not mean to, but get provoked into saying a little more than we intended; and friends, once it's on the Web, it exists forever. A little MOUTHSEC could go a long way. It is possible to be friends with someone and disagree on big issues. But insulting remarks and harsh commentary is not soon forgotten. It places a wall between us that doesn't need to exist. We can be opinionated and also quiet. It is a rare creature, but exists indeed.

Reflection:

What is one concrete way I will choose to live in peace with others?

Homecoming

Every parting is a form of death, as every
reunion is a type of heaven.
                                                  –Tryon Edwards

Day 100

From time to time, I have friends who come to me and share their marital troubles. There are many issues that arise, from finances to insensitivity, but one underlying problem seems to be intimacy. A problem leads to an argument and grudges, and suddenly, the couple is not being intimate like they used to. Many things can contribute to this. The biggest is probably having children. I know I sometimes feel like I have a symbiotic relationship with my children who always seemed to be attached to me with super glue. When I put them to bed, I need to decompress. I need some space. Here's the problem, my husband needs me, too. God made him to be a physical creature who connects emotionally by being physical. Matthew 19:5 says, "Therefore a man shall leave his father and his mother and hold fast to his wife, and the two shall become one flesh."

So many times, we don't feel sexy. We may be carrying some extra weight from our last kid, or missed our shower because of a cranky baby. We may have been puked on several times this week. I get it. You think you're not sexy in this stage of life. But do you know what is sexy to your husband? Having sex. If his needs are being met, he is not even thinking about your pudgy waistline, trust me on that. This is something to consider when our husbands return. At first, there will be romance. You will be so glad to see him, but soon, the intimacy may dwindle as you settle back into routine. I urge you to take the time to be romantic still. Plan a date night away from the kids, send suggestive messages to him, or buy a cute nightie. Keep it exciting! As far as arguments go, I firmly believe that discussions are more productive when couples are connected through intimacy. What may have turned into an argument may just be a conversation when you are both feeling loved and connected to one another.

Reflection:

How can I make a concerted effort to connect romantically with my husband?

Day 101

After the death of Christ, a deep sadness settled on the disciples and other followers of Jesus. They were confused and heartbroken. Imagine the excitement they felt when, as they were fishing days later, a man called out to them, and they realized it was their risen Lord. In a dramatic display of love and excitement, Peter jumped right into the water with his clothes on and started swimming to shore so he could hug him faster.

I can't say I've been tempted to jump into the water when I've seen my husband's ship coming to shore, but it's only because I had spent so much time picking out the perfect dress and woke up in the wee hours of the morning to do my hair. You can relate to Peter's excitement, I'm sure. Homecomings are full of anticipation, and when you catch that first glimpse of your man, there is no greater feeling. He's finally home. All is well.

Jesus didn't tell them everything would be perfect, though. He warned the disciples that they would face hardships, and military families can count on hardships in the future as well. Getting used to being a family again can be tough. We think it will be like a Disney movie, and we will all live happily ever after, but the truth is, it may take a little while to get back into the swing of things. Truthfully, after my husband has been gone for an extended time, I feel like I have to get to know him again. Even holding hands feels awkward and nervous. Feeling normal again will come with time. There is a shifting of roles as you begin to hand over some of the responsibilities you have been taking care of. Maybe you are not ready to give up the reigns. Sometimes, there is a struggle with the kids, and they push the boundaries.

Despite all this, the God who got your through this deployment will be with you while you put your family back together. When the disciples were worried, Jesus told them, "I have said these things to you, that in me you may have peace. In the world you will have tribulation. But take heart; I have overcome the world" (John 16:33). Likewise, we can have peace that, even when we struggle, God is with us. He will help form us into a family again!

Reflection:

What do I foresee as being problem areas when my husband returns, and how can I address these in a healthy way?

Day 102

You will make some of the most lasting friendships you have as a military wife. No one can understand what you have been through except other military wives. Especially when you are sharing a deployment together, you will get very close, even like sisters. One of my Navy sisters and I were gearing up for homecoming, and were beside ourselves with the thought of having our husbands back. We were daydreaming about all the things that would be once they returned. Maybe we'll take a romantic trip, we mused. Perhaps, it's time to start our family, we thought. We will finally have someone to mow the lawn, we sighed. One thing that never popped into our heads were our in-laws.

Oh yeah, those people who also care about our husbands and have missed him too. Hmm. That kind of throws a kink in things. My friend's MIL thought it was totally appropriate to be on the pier when the ship came in and then retire at their home, where she would spend a week catching up with her son. She was completely oblivious to the reconnection that was necessary for husband and wife. And by "reconnection" I mean the copious amounts of sex to make up for lost time. How could this lady be so dense? It ended up being a bit of family drama before it was all hammered out, and everyone's feelings were sufficiently hurt.

It may be wise to have a bit of a talk with your husband about what he envisions homecoming to be. It may be necessary to spell out to the in-laws what you've decided as a couple, and have your husband deliver the news, if possible. I have three boys of my own, and I can imagine wanting to run down the pier, pushing women and children out of my way to plant a smoochie on my boy after he's been in harm's way for months, so I understand the urge. However, I also believe that homecoming is a very special time for the husband and wife. It is smart to lay down some ground rules when homecoming comes around. What compromise are you willing to make? Maybe MIL and FIL can come to the homecoming and stay in a hotel for a couple of days. Maybe they are invited to a "welcome home" party a week after he gets back. That is for you and your hubby to decide.

"Let all bitterness and wrath and anger and clamor and slander be put away from you, along with all malice. Be kind to one another, tenderhearted, forgiving one another, as God in Christ forgave you" (Eph. 4:31–32).

Reflection:

How do I envision homecoming? What does my husband want it to be like? How can we honor those in our families while keeping healthy boundaries?

CPSIA information can be obtained
at www.ICGtesting.com
Printed in the USA
LVHW041156240123
737819LV00002B/267